The *Junior* cook

Step-by-Step

The *Junior* cook

FUN
Step-by-Step

bay books

Fried Rice, page 41

CONTENTS

The test kitchen is where our recipes are double-tested by our team of home economists to ensure a high standard of success and delicious results every time.

After testing, recipes are rated for ease of preparation and given one of the following cookery ratings in this book.

✲

A single Cooking with Confidence symbol indicates that this recipe is simple and fairly quick to make, perfect for beginners.

✲ ✲

Two symbols indicate the need for a little more care and time.

✲ ✲ ✲

Three symbols indicate special dishes that require more time, care and patience, but the results are worth it.

A selection of easy-to-make muffins, page 94

Bean nachos, page 50

HOW TO

A FEW TIPS, TERMS AND IDEAS WHICH WILL
HAVE YOU COOKING CONFIDENTLY IN NO TIME

INTRODUCTION

So you want to learn to cook? This book is the ultimate guide for making everything from a simple snack to dinner for the family to a show-stopping dessert, with a batch of biscuits along the way. You may need an adult to help you with some of the tricky bits, but don't let them take all the credit for your scrumptious creations.

Don't worry if adults are a little reluctant to let you loose in the kitchen at first—once you've served up your first successes, they'll probably be begging you to make dinner every day.

We've tried to give traditional versions of most recipes, so you know how they *should* be prepared. This means some dishes may contain alcohol, which, depending on who you're cooking for, you may or may not want to include. If you prefer, use stock in a savoury recipe. Small amounts can be left out altogether. When alcohol is cooked, it loses its alcoholic content but keeps its flavour.

GETTING STARTED

The real secret to being a good cook is to be an organised cook. This means reading through the recipe fully before starting, and assembling all the ingredients and equipment you are going to need. There is nothing worse than getting halfway through a recipe, realising that you are missing a crucial ingredient and having to bribe your little brother to go on an emergency shopping trip.

Don't forget to preheat the oven and prepare the cooking dish, if necessary. Do any preparation that can be done first, such as peeling, chopping or grating vegetables.

Try to avoid being interrupted or distracted. Keep referring to the recipe as you go, double checking that all the ingredients have been added at the right time, and keeping on top of what has to be done next. Have a kitchen timer or clock nearby, so you can time the stages accurately. And remember, try to wash up as you go along. It will save hours of cleaning at the end and keeps your work space clear.

MEASURING

When you've been cooking for a while you can start to estimate quantities fairly accurately, but this takes experience. An inaccurate measurement, especially when baking, can mean the difference between disaster and success. Measure everything carefully. If a recipe asks for a cup of something, say flour, it means a proper measuring cup, not something you drink tea from. A set of spoon measures is also necessary—don't be tempted to grab any old spoon from the cutlery drawer.

SHOPPING AND STORAGE TIPS

There are 3 main areas for storing food: the pantry, the refrigerator and the freezer. Most 'dry' ingredients will keep well in the pantry, which should be dark, cool and dry. It is a good idea to transfer the contents of packets into airtight containers once opened, especially in humid areas where weevils can be a problem. Canned food will keep for months, provided the cans are not rusted or damaged. Foods in bottles and jars, such as pickles, jams and mustards, should be refrigerated after opening. Buy infrequently used ingredients, including ground spices, in small quantities. Check use-by dates and have regular cleanouts; that way you will always know what you have

and how fresh it is. Be ruthless and throw out anything that looks suspect, particularly in the refrigerator or freezer.

● Meat will keep for up to 3 days in the refrigerator, and up to 6 months in the freezer. To freeze meat, wrap each piece tightly in plastic wrap, then place it in a freezer bag, expelling all the air. Label and date the bag. To thaw, place it on a large plate and leave it in the refrigerator—never thaw it at room temperature or under water. Do not re-freeze thawed meat unless you cook it first.

● Chicken should be treated with a lot of care as it can harbour salmonella bacteria. Refrigerate it for a maximum of 2 days or freeze it for up to 6 months. Thaw chicken in the same way as meat, and cook it within 12 hours of thawing. Never let the raw chicken come into contact with other foods in the refrigerator.

● Vegetables can be kept in the crisper compartment of the refrigerator. Leafy vegetables will stay crisp if you wash and dry them, then seal them in a large plastic bag (don't expel the air). Keep potatoes and onions in a cool, dark place, with some ventilation. The best tip is to buy vegetables every couple of days. This way you avoid waste and know that your vegetables are fresh. You could also try growing your own—many things can be grown in pots, even in the smallest space.

SAFETY POINTS

Here are a few hints and tips to make cooking safe and enjoyable.

● Always ask an adult for permission before you start to cook.
● Before starting to cook, wash your hands well with soap and water.
● Wear an apron to protect your clothes and wear closed-in, non-slip shoes to protect your feet.
● For very young cooks, ask an adult to help you chop things. Never cut directly on a kitchen surface—always use a chopping board.
● Always use oven gloves when moving anything in or out of the oven.
● Turn saucepan handles to the side when cooking so you don't knock them.
● Never use electrical appliances near water. Always have dry hands before you start to use any appliance.
● Be very careful with pots and pans on the stove. Never reach across a hot saucepan of food—steam is very hot and can cause a nasty burn.

5

KNOW YOUR COOKERY TERMS

BOIL—to have a mixture (usually liquid) cooking at boiling point. The surface will be bubbling and moving fairly vigourously. To quickly bring a mixture to the boil, cover with a lid. Uncover as soon as it begins to boil, or it may boil over and make a mess.

BAKE—to cook in the oven, which should always be preheated to the required temperature before the food goes in. If you are unsure of the accuracy of your oven, buy an oven thermometer and leave it in your oven.

BEAT—to work a mixture together, using electric beaters or sometimes a wooden spoon. This is to combine ingredients and sometimes to incorporate air, as for egg whites.

FOLD—to combine ingredients very gently. Use a large metal spoon or rubber spatula and scoop and turn the mixture, without beating, until combined.

MARINATE—to soak food, usually meat, in a sauce-type mixture (marinade) which will flavour or tenderise it.

SIFT—to put dry ingredients through mesh. This removes lumps and unwanted particles, and adds air which will lighten the finished product.

SIMMER—to have a mixture (usually liquid) cooking at a slow boil over low heat. The surface will be slightly bubbling.

STEAM—to cook vegetables over, rather than in, a pan of boiling water.

HOW TO COOK PASTA

Use the biggest pan you have. For every 500 g (1 lb) of pasta, you will need at least 4 litres of water. Overcrowding the pan will make the pasta clump together and cook unevenly. Bring the water to the boil, add the pasta and give

Test the pasta by tasting it just before the given time. Cook a bit longer if necessary.

it a brief stir. The water will stop boiling, so cover the pan and bring it back to the boil. As soon as it boils, take off the lid and begin timing. The cooking times will vary according to the brand, size and shape of the pasta, so check the packet for instructions. Just before the given time, take out a piece of pasta and taste it. If it is not ready, keeping tasting every couple of minutes. The pasta will be done when it is

tender yet firm, with no raw taste. This is what is know as 'al dente'. Drain the pasta and use as directed in the recipe.

HOW TO COOK RICE

Rice can be cooked by a number of methods, the most common being the 'rapid boil' method and the 'absorption' method. The rapid boil method is a quick and relatively foolproof method of cooking rice, but the rice can tend to be a little gluggy. Bring a large pan of water to the boil, add the rice and return to the boil. Cook for about 12 minutes, or until the rice is tender, then drain well in a colander. (Brown rice will take about 40 minutes to cook.)

Cooking rice by the absorption method takes a little practice, but results in deliciously light, fluffy rice if done properly. Place 2 cups (400 g/12$\frac{2}{3}$ oz) of long-grain white rice into a sieve and rinse under cold running water until the water runs clear. Set aside to drain. Put 3 cups (750 ml/24 fl oz) water in a medium pan, cover and bring to the boil. As soon as the

Rice cooked by the absorption method should be rinsed first, to remove excess starch.

water boils, add the rice and stir it once to distribute the grains. Put the lid back on and return to the boil. Reduce the heat to as low as possible, and cook for 7–10 minutes, or until the water is nearly all absorbed into the rice. Turn off the heat and leave the rice to steam for another 5 minutes. Fluff up the rice with a fork and serve.

HOW TO MAKE A PAPER PIPING BAG

Part of the fun of baking cakes, slices and biscuits is decorating them. To pipe fine lines, you will need to make a paper piping bag. Alternatively you can use a small plastic bag with the corner snipped off.

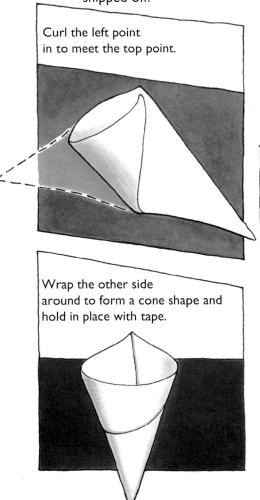

Curl the left point in to meet the top point.

Wrap the other side around to form a cone shape and hold in place with tape.

Cut a sheet of greaseproof paper 25 cm (10 inches) square. You can use baking paper but it is a little more difficult for first attempts. Fold the paper in half diagonally to form a triangle. Working with the long side nearest you, curl the left point in to meet the top point. Hold in place while wrapping the other side around tightly to form a snug cone shape. Hold in place with tape. Tuck the upstanding ends into the cone. Fill with melted chocolate or icing mixture, and fold the top edges down to seal. Snip the tip off the end. To use, gently apply pressure from the top of the bag.

HOW TO MAKE FRESH BREADCRUMBS

Some recipes ask for dry breadcrumbs, which means the ones you buy in packets. If the recipe asks for fresh breadcrumbs, you will need to make them yourself.

Tear the bread into pieces and put into a food processor.

Remove the crusts from slices of day-old white bread, and tear the bread into pieces. Put the pieces into a food processor, and process in short bursts until breadcrumbs have formed. Fresh breadcrumbs are a lot bigger and fluffier than dry breadcrumbs. For 1 cup (80 g/2⅔ oz) of fresh breadcrumbs you will need 5 slices of bread. Making fresh breadcrumbs is a good way to use up day-old bread; sealed in a freezer bag they can be frozen for up to 3 months.

HOW TO MAKE STOCK

Stock is available in different forms. The one you choose will be a matter of taste and convenience. Stock is available in long-life cartons from supermarkets or in cubes or powder. Cubes or powder dissolved in 1 cup (250 ml/8 fl oz) of water will make 1 cup of stock. Check the package for the amount of stock to add to the water. The best stock, however, is homemade. This can be frozen in convenient portions for later use. Remember that commercial stock is much saltier than homemade, so always taste the finished dish before adding salt and pepper.

1 Preheat the oven to moderate 180°C (350°F/Gas 4). Put 1.5 kg (3 lb) chicken bones or beef bones and 2 chopped unpeeled onions into a large baking dish, and bake for about 45 minutes, or until well browned. Turn with tongs occasionally during cooking. When ready, transfer to a large heavy-based pan.

2 Add 2 roughly chopped unpeeled carrots, 2 chopped sticks of celery with their leaves, 12 whole black peppercorns and 3 litres of water. Also add a

Place the bones and onions in a large baking dish, and bake until well browned.

bouquet garni, which is a sprig of parsley, a sprig of thyme and a bay leaf wrapped together in a small piece of muslin.

3 Bring slowly to the boil, then immediately reduce the heat and gently simmer, uncovered, for 3 hours. Skim any froth that forms on the surface. Cool the stock slightly, then strain it through a fine sieve into a bowl.

Strain the stock through a fine sieve, into a bowl.

4 Chill the stock in the refrigerator and remove any fat that sets on the top. Keep in the refrigerator for up to 7 days, or freeze for up to 6 months.
Note: To make vegetable stock, use the same method from Step 2 but use 4 onions, 5 carrots, 2 parsnips, 5 celery sticks, a bouquet garni and 12 peppercorns. Simmer all the

ingredients in 3 litres of water for 1 hour, or until the liquid is reduced by half. Strain and store as directed above.

HOW TO LINE A ROUND CAKE TIN

We use baking paper, which is non-stick, to line cake tins. You can use ordinary greaseproof paper but it must be brushed with melted butter or oil after lining the tin. Square tins are easy to line, but round ones can be tricky, so follow the instructions.

1 Tear off a sheet of baking paper which is square and a little larger than the tin. Sit the tin on the paper, and draw a circle around the outside of the tin.

2 Lightly brush the tin with oil or melted butter. This makes the paper stay in place.

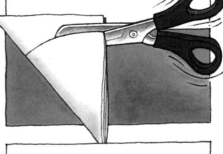

Fold the paper into triangles 4 times, and cut along the line.

Make a crease along one edge of the paper, then make cuts to the fold mark, about 1 cm (¹/2 inch) apart.

3 Fold the paper into triangles 4 times, keeping the line together, then cut along the line. Unfold the paper circle.

4 Cut a strip of baking paper long enough to go around the inside of the tin and to overlap slightly. Make the strip about 2 cm (³/4 inch) wider than the height of the tin. Make a crease 2 cm (³/4 inch) from one long edge of the paper, then make cuts to the crease mark, about 1 cm (¹/2 inch) apart. Line the inside of the tin with the strip, with the crease around the bottom and the cut edge sitting flat on the base. Place the circle of paper into the base.

HOW TO BOIL AN EGG

Add enough water to a pan so it is three-quarters full. Add the eggs gently. The eggs are less likely to crack if they are at room temperature, not straight from

To stop the eggs cracking, lower them into the pan on a spoon.

the fridge. Place over medium–high heat, and as soon as the water starts to boil, begin timing. Allow 8 minutes for hard-boiled eggs, and 3 minutes for soft-boiled eggs. When cooked, lift from the pan with a spoon.

HOW TO PEEL GARLIC

Place a clove of garlic on a board. Lay a knife with a wide blade on the garlic, and give it a firm whack with the heel of your hand. The papery skin will come away easily.

Hit the side of the blade with the heel of your hand.

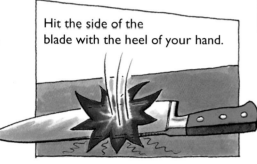

HOW TO MAKE GRAVY

Once your roasted meat is ready, it's time to make the gravy.
1 Sprinkle 2 tablespoons of plain flour onto a baking tray. Place the tray under a preheated moderate grill for about 5 minutes, or until the flour turns golden brown. Stir the flour occasionally so it browns evenly. This adds colour and flavour to the gravy.
2 Remove the roasted meat from the baking dish and set it

Cook the flour until it browns, stirring occasionally.

Add the stock gradually, stirring until smooth between each addition.

aside, covered with foil. Place the baking dish on top of the stove over medium-low heat and sprinkle the toasted flour over the pan juices. Stir with a wooden spoon until a smooth paste is formed, and cook for 2 minutes, stirring constantly.
3 You will need about 2 cups (500 ml/16 fl oz) of stock, depending on how thin you would like the gravy (use chicken, beef or vegetable stock). Add the stock a little at a time, stirring so the mixture is smooth between each addition. If you add more stock before stirring any lumps out, they are there for good!
4 When all the stock has been added, bring to the boil, reduce the heat slightly and cook for 1 more minute, still stirring. Season with salt and pepper to taste, and transfer to a warm jug to serve with the meat.

HOW TO BEAT EGG WHITES

Achieving full, frothy peaks is easy if you follow a few basic rules:
● Always use clean, dry equipment. If the bowl or beaters have any grease on them at all, the egg whites may stay flat no matter how long or hard you beat them.
● Use the size of bowl indicated in the recipe. Beating 1 or 2 egg whites in a huge bowl will find you simply chasing them around the bowl. The same goes when creaming a small amount of butter and sugar.
● When adding sugar, as for meringue, beat the whites to soft peaks before adding any sugar. Add the sugar gradually, a tablespoon at a time at first, and beat until dissolved between each addition (test between your thumb and forefinger for grittiness). The sugar can be added in larger quantities as you go along.

Add the sugar gradually at first, beating until completely dissolved between each addition.

What is meant by soft peaks? The egg whites are beaten until the mixture just holds its shape; the tips of the peaks will gently curl over.
What is meant by stiff peaks? The mixture becomes quite firm and the peaks stand up. Take care not to overbeat at this stage, otherwise the mixture will separate.

SENSATIONAL SOUPS

WITH A NOURISHING BOWL OF SOUP, A SALAD AND SOME BREAD YOU HAVE AN EASY, COMPLETE MEAL

MINESTRONE SOUP

Preparation time: 30 minutes
Total cooking time: 40 minutes
Serves 4

★ ★

1 tablespoon oil

1 onion, chopped

1 rasher bacon, chopped

1 clove garlic, crushed

1.25 litres beef stock (page 7)

2 tomatoes, chopped

1 carrot, chopped

1 potato, chopped

1 celery stick, chopped

2 tablespoons tomato paste

1 zucchini (courgette), sliced

100 g (3 1/3 oz) green beans, chopped

1/3 cup (50 g/1 2/3 oz) macaroni

2 tablespoons chopped fresh parsley

300 g (9 2/3 oz) can red kidney beans

finely grated Parmesan cheese, to serve

1 Heat the oil in a large pan and cook the onion and bacon until lightly browned. Add the garlic and cook for 1 minute more.

2 Add the stock, tomato, carrot, potato, celery and tomato paste to the pan. Bring to the boil, reduce the heat and simmer for 20 minutes.

3 Add the zucchini, green beans, macaroni and parsley to the pan; simmer for a further 15 minutes. Rinse and drain the kidney beans and add to the pan.

4 Ladle the soup into serving bowls, sprinkle the Parmesan cheese on top. Serve immediately.

NOTE

Minestrone is a great way of using any leftover vegetables. Also any small pasta shapes can be used when making minestrone; look out for cartoon character pasta shapes. Canned butter beans or borlotti beans can be substituted for the kidney beans.

CHICKEN NOODLE SOUP

Preparation time: 20 minutes
Total cooking time:
15 minutes
Serves 4–6

★

2 litres chicken stock (page 7)

1 cup (175 g/5²⁄₃ oz) finely shredded cooked chicken

150 g (4³⁄₄ oz) vermicelli

½ cup (30 g/1 oz) chopped parsley

1 Put the stock into a large pan, and bring to the boil. It will boil more quickly if you put a lid on the pan.

2 Add the shredded chicken to the pan, and simmer for 1–2 minutes to heat through.

3 Break the vermicelli into pieces and add it to the pan. Cook for a further 5 minutes, until the noodles are tender.

4 Stir the parsley through the soup, and serve immediately.

NOTE Use purchased BBQ chicken for this recipe, or lightly pan-fry a small breast fillet in a little butter until golden and cooked through. Vermicelli noodles look like spaghetti but they are much thinner.

HEARTY VEGETABLE SOUP

Preparation time: 25 minutes
+ 8 hours soaking
Total cooking time: 55 minutes
Serves 6

⭐

1 cup (220 g/7 oz) dried soup mix

2 tablespoons oil

1 large onion, finely chopped

1 green pepper (capsicum),
chopped

2 zucchinis (courgettes), sliced

2 celery sticks, sliced

125 g (4 oz) mushrooms, sliced

2 carrots, peeled and sliced

1 large potato, peeled and chopped

500 g (1 lb) pumpkin, peeled
and chopped

2 litres vegetable stock

1 Put the soup mix in a large bowl and cover it with cold water. Leave to soak for 8 hours.

2 Heat the oil in a large pan and cook the onion until soft and lightly golden. Add the green pepper, zucchini, celery and mushrooms and stir-fry for about 5 minutes.

3 Add the carrot, potato and pumpkin and stir to combine. Pour in the stock.

4 Drain the soup mix and add to the pan. Bring to the boil, then reduce the heat.

5 Partially cover the pan with a lid, and simmer for about 45 minutes, or until the vegetables and soup mix are very soft.

NOTE Dried soup mix is a combination of split peas, barley, lentils and dried beans. It is available from supermarkets and health food shops.

PEA AND HAM SOUP

Preparation time:
20 minutes + soaking
Total cooking time:
2 hours 30 minutes
Serves 4–6

★★

2 cups (440 g/14 oz) green
split peas

750 g (1 ½ lb) ham bones

2.5 litres water

1 celery stick, including
top, chopped

1 carrot, chopped

1 onion, chopped

3 leeks, sliced

1 potato, chopped

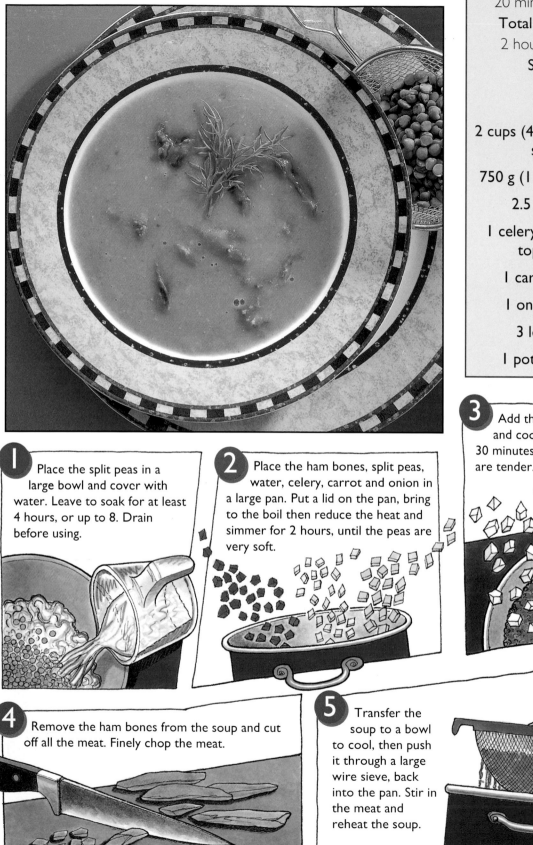

3 Add the leek and potato, and cook for another 30 minutes, until the vegetables are tender.

1 Place the split peas in a large bowl and cover with water. Leave to soak for at least 4 hours, or up to 8. Drain before using.

2 Place the ham bones, split peas, water, celery, carrot and onion in a large pan. Put a lid on the pan, bring to the boil then reduce the heat and simmer for 2 hours, until the peas are very soft.

4 Remove the ham bones from the soup and cut off all the meat. Finely chop the meat.

5 Transfer the soup to a bowl to cool, then push it through a large wire sieve, back into the pan. Stir in the meat and reheat the soup.

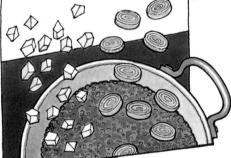

FRENCH ONION SOUP

Preparation time:
15 minutes
Total cooking time:
1 hour 15 minutes
Serves 4–6

★

6 onions (approx 1 kg/2 lb)

60 g (2 oz) butter

1 teaspoon sugar

¼ cup (30 g/1 oz) plain flour

2 litres beef stock (page 7)

1 stick French bread

½ cup (60 g/2 oz) grated Cheddar cheese

1 Peel the onions and cut them into fine rings.

2 Heat the butter in a large pan, add the onion and cook over low heat for 20 minutes, or until the onion is golden brown and very soft.

3 Add the sugar and the flour to the pan and cook, stirring, for 1–2 minutes, or until the mixture is just starting to turn golden.

4 Gradually stir in the stock and bring to the boil. Reduce the heat and simmer, covered, for 1 hour. Season with salt and pepper to taste.

5 Cut the breadstick into 2 cm (³/₄ inch) slices and arrange them on a baking tray. Cook under a preheated hot grill until golden on one side. Turn the slices over and sprinkle each slice with some of the grated cheese. Cook under a hot grill until the cheese has melted. Serve the soup topped with the grilled cheese toasts.

PUMPKIN SOUP

Preparation time: 25 minutes
Total cooking time: 40 minutes
Serves 4-6

★

1 kg (2 lb) piece of pumpkin

60 g (2 oz) butter

1 onion, chopped

1 litre chicken stock (page 7)

3/4 cup (185 ml/6 fl oz) cream

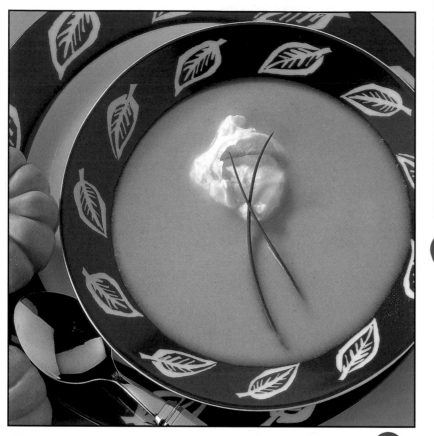

1 Cut the pumpkin into large manageable pieces, then cut off all the skin. Chop into smaller pieces. This can be a very difficult and sometimes dangerous task, and is best done by an adult.

2 Heat the butter in a large pan, add the onion and cook gently for 15 minutes, or until the onion is very soft.

3 Add the pumpkin and stock to the pan. Put a lid on the pan and bring to the boil, then reduce the heat and simmer for 20 minutes, or until the pumpkin is tender.

4 At this stage you can mash the soup mixture thoroughly with a potato masher, or, for a very smooth texture, purée the soup in a food processor or blender.

5 Let the soup cool before placing it in a processor. Purée in small batches so the liquid does not overflow when being blended.

6 Return the soup to the pan (if it has been puréed), and add the cream, and salt and pepper to taste. Stir over low heat until heated through; serve with sour cream, if you like.

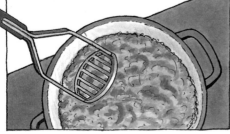

CREAM OF TOMATO SOUP

Preparation time:
15 minutes
Total cooking time:
25 minutes
Serves 4

★

1 tablespoon olive oil

1 onion, finely chopped

2 cloves garlic, crushed

3 x 410 g (13 oz) cans crushed tomatoes

3 cups (750 ml/24 fl oz) chicken stock (page 7)

1 tablespoon tomato paste

2 teaspoons soft brown sugar

1 cup (250 ml/8 fl oz) cream

1 Heat the oil in a large pan. Add the onion and cook until very soft and lightly golden, stirring occasionally. Add the garlic and cook for 1 more minute.

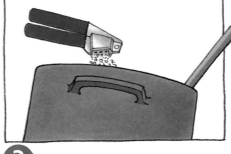

2 Add the tomatoes, stock, tomato paste and sugar to the pan. Bring to the boil then reduce the heat.

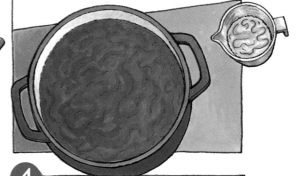

3 Simmer the soup, partially covered with a lid, for 20 minutes. Allow the soup to cool a little, then process it in batches in a blender or food processor until smooth.

4 Return the soup to the pan, stir in the cream and reheat gently. Don't let the soup boil once you have added the cream, or it will curdle.

DINNER FOR FRIENDS

IMPRESS YOUR FAMILY AND FRIENDS BY RUSTLING UP ONE OF THESE GREAT DINNERS— BE PREPARED FOR REQUESTS FOR SECONDS

ROAST SEASONED CHICKEN

Preparation time: 30 minutes
Total cooking time:
1 hour 40 minutes
Serves 4

★

1 x 1.5 kg (3 lb) chicken

45 g (1 1/2 oz) butter

2 rashers bacon, finely chopped

1 medium onion, finely chopped

1 celery stick, finely chopped

1 2/3 cups (135 g/4 1/2 oz) fresh breadcrumbs

1 egg, lightly beaten

3 tablespoons finely chopped parsley

2 tablespoons freshly chopped lemon thyme or sage

1 tablespoon oil

a squeeze of lemon juice

1 Preheat the oven to moderate 180°C (350°F/Gas 4). Cut away any loose fat from the chicken. Rinse well and pat dry with paper towels. If the chicken has been frozen and thawed, it will be necessary to dry the inside cavity as well.

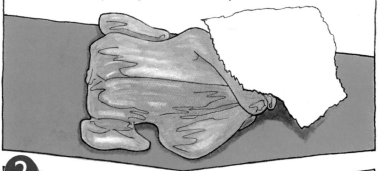

2 Heat 20 g (2/3 oz) of the butter in a frying pan. Add the bacon and cook over medium heat until browned and crisp. Remove and drain on paper towels. Add the onion and celery and cook until softened.

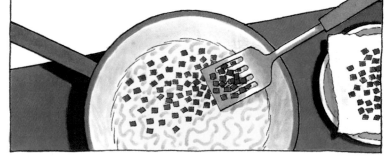

3 Combine the bacon, onion and celery mixture in a bowl. Add the breadcrumbs, egg, parsley and thyme or sage. You may wish to add a little grated lemon rind to this mixture. Mix well. Add some salt and pepper.

4 Bend the wing tips back and tuck them under the chicken (so they don't burn). Stuff the seasoning into the cavity.

5 Tie or skewer the legs together to close the cavity. Place the chicken on a roasting rack in a baking dish. Add a little water to the base of the dish; this will help to keep the chicken moist as it cooks.

6 Melt the remaining butter and mix with the oil, lemon juice and some salt and pepper. Brush this all over the chicken and bake for 1 hour 25–30 minutes, or until golden and the chicken juices run clear when the thickest part of the thigh is pierced with a skewer. Cover the chicken with foil and allow to stand for at least 5 minutes before carving. Serve with gravy (see page 9 for recipe) and roast vegetables (see page 38 for recipe).

SPAGHETTI BOLOGNESE

Preparation time:
15 minutes
Total cooking time:
1 hour 40 minutes
Serves 4–6

★

2 tablespoons olive oil

1 large onion, finely
chopped

1 medium carrot, finely
chopped

1 celery stick, finely
chopped

2 cloves garlic, crushed

500 g (1 lb) beef mince

2 cups (500 ml/16 fl oz)
beef stock (page 7)

1 cup (250 ml/8 fl oz) red
wine

800 g (1 lb 10 oz) can
crushed tomatoes

2 tablespoons chopped
fresh parsley

500 g (1 lb) spaghetti

Parmesan cheese,
to serve

1 Heat the oil in a large pan. Add the onion, carrot and celery. Cook until the onion is soft and lightly golden, stirring occasionally. Add the garlic and cook 1 more minute.

2 Add the mince to the pan, and break it up with a fork as it cooks. When it is well browned, add the stock, wine, undrained tomatoes and parsley.

5 Top the spaghetti with the Bolognese sauce, and sprinkle it with the Parmesan cheese. Serve immediately.

3 Bring to the boil, reduce the heat to very low and simmer, uncovered, for about 1 1/2 hours, stirring occasionally. Season to taste with salt and pepper.

4 Cook the spaghetti in a large pan of boiling water until just tender (about 12 minutes). Drain well and divide among serving bowls.

PENNE WITH VEGETABLES

Preparation time: 20 minutes
Total cooking time: 15 minutes
Serves 4

★

500 g (1 lb) penne

3 tablespoons olive oil

3 zucchinis (courgettes), sliced

2 cloves garlic, crushed

3 spring onions, chopped

1 red pepper (capsicum), cut into strips

1/3 cup (65 g/2 1/4 oz) corn kernels

3 tomatoes, chopped

2 tablespoons chopped fresh parsley

1 Add the penne to a large pan of boiling water and cook until just tender (about 12 minutes).

2 Heat 2 tablespoons of the oil in a large frying pan, add the zucchini and cook, stirring, for 3 minutes.

3 Add the garlic, spring onion, red pepper and corn to the pan, and stir-fry for a further 2–3 minutes.

4 Stir the tomato into the vegetable mixture and set aside.

5 Drain the pasta in a colander, then return it to the pan. Add the parsley and remaining oil, and toss to combine.

6 Divide the pasta among serving bowls and top with the vegetables. Serve immediately.

LASAGNE

Preparation time:
30 minutes

Total cooking time:
1 hour 15 minutes

Serves 4-6

★★ ☆

250 g (8 oz) packet instant lasagne sheets

1/2 cup (75 g/2 1/2 oz) grated mozzarella cheese

1/2 cup (60 g/2 oz) grated Cheddar cheese

1/2 cup (125 ml/4 fl oz) cream

1/4 cup (25 g/3/4 oz) freshly grated Parmesan cheese

Cheese Sauce

60 g (2 oz) butter

1/3 cup (40 g/1 1/3 oz) plain flour

2 cups (500 ml/16 fl oz) milk

1 cup (125 g/4 oz) grated Cheddar cheese

Meat Sauce

1 tablespoon olive oil

1 onion, finely chopped

1 clove garlic, crushed

500 g (1 lb) beef mince

800 g (1 lb 10 oz) can crushed tomatoes

1/4 cup (60 ml/2 fl oz) red wine

1 teaspoon dried oregano leaves

1 teaspoon dried basil leaves

1 Preheat the oven to moderate 180°C (350°F/Gas 4). Brush a shallow ovenproof dish (about 23 x 30 cm/9 x 12 inches) with a little oil. Line with 1 layer of lasagne sheets, breaking them to fill any gaps as necessary.

2 **To make Cheese Sauce:** Melt the butter in a medium pan. Add the flour and cook, stirring, for 1 minute, until golden and bubbling.

3 Add the milk a little at a time, stirring until smooth between each addition. Bring to the boil, still stirring, and reduce the heat. Simmer, uncovered, for 2 minutes.

4 Remove the pan from the heat, add the cheese and stir until melted and smooth. Season with salt and pepper.

5 **To make Meat Sauce:** Heat the oil in a large pan. Add the onion and cook until soft and lightly golden, stirring occasionally. Add the garlic and cook for 1 more minute.

6 Add the mince to the pan, and break it up with a fork as it cooks. When it is well browned, add the undrained tomatoes, wine and herbs. Reduce the heat and simmer for 20 minutes.

7 Spoon one-third of the Meat Sauce over the lasagne sheets, and top with one-third of the Cheese Sauce.

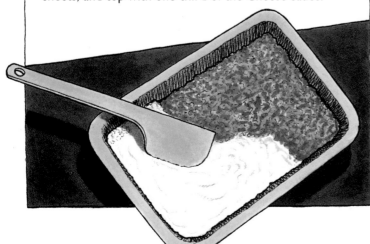

8 Continue layering, finishing with lasagne sheets. Sprinkle with the combined mozzarella and Cheddar cheeses. Pour the cream all over the top, and sprinkle with the Parmesan. Bake for 35–40 minutes, or until golden brown.

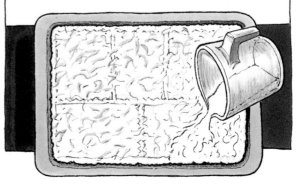

MACARONI CHEESE

Preparation time:
15 minutes
Total cooking time:
35 minutes
Serves 4

★ ★

60 g (2 oz) butter

2 tablespoons plain flour

2 cups (500 ml/16 fl oz) milk

1 cup (250 ml/8 fl oz) cream

2 cups (250 g/8 oz) grated Cheddar cheese

1/2 cup (50 g/1 2/3 oz) freshly grated Parmesan cheese

375 g (12 oz) macaroni

1 cup (80 g/2 2/3 oz) fresh breadcrumbs

---

1 Preheat the oven to moderate 180°C (350°F/Gas 4). Melt the butter in a medium pan. Add the flour and cook for 1 minute, stirring, until golden and bubbling.

2 Combine the milk and cream, and add to the pan a little at a time, stirring until smooth between each addition.

3 Bring to the boil, still stirring, and reduce the heat. Simmer, uncovered, for 2 minutes.

4 Remove from the heat and add half the Cheddar and Parmesan cheese. Stir until melted and smooth.

5 Meanwhile, cook the macaroni in a large pan of boiling water until just tender (about 12 minutes). Drain well and return to the pan. Add the cheese sauce and stir until well combined.

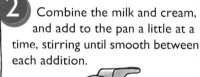

6 Spoon into a deep casserole dish. Sprinkle with the combined breadcrumbs and remaining cheese. Bake for 15–20 minutes, or until golden.

FETTUCINE CARBONARA

Preparation time: 10 minutes
Total cooking time: 25 minutes
Serves 4

8 rashers bacon

2 teaspoons oil

500 g (1 lb) fettucine

4 eggs

$^1/_2$ cup (50 g/1$^2/_3$ oz) freshly grated Parmesan cheese

1 cup (250 ml/8 fl oz) cream

1 Remove and discard the rind from the bacon. Cut the bacon into thin strips.

2 Heat the oil in a frying pan and cook the bacon over medium heat until brown and crisp. Remove from the pan and drain on paper towels.

4 While the pasta is cooking, put the eggs, cheese and cream into a small bowl or jug and beat together with a fork. Add the bacon to the mixture.

5 Pour the sauce over the hot pasta and return the pan to the stove. Stir over very low heat for a minute, until the sauce thickens. Serve immediately with freshly ground black pepper.

3 Add the fettucine to a large pan of boiling water and cook until just tender (about 12 minutes). Drain well in a colander, then return it to the pan.

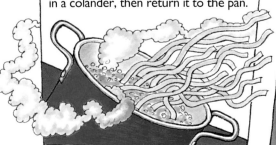

COTTAGE PIE

Preparation time: 30 minutes
Total cooking time: 50 minutes
Serves 2–4

★

2 tablespoons olive oil

30 g (1 oz) butter

1 kg (2 lb) lean beef mince or finely chopped lean beef

1 large onion, chopped

1 large carrot, diced

½ cup (125 ml/4 fl oz) tomato sauce

¼ cup (60 ml/2 fl oz) beef or vegetable stock (page 7)

425 g (13½ oz) can crushed tomatoes

¾ cup (115 g/3¾ oz) peas

3 large potatoes (about 1 kg)

30 g (1 oz) butter, extra

1–2 tablespoons milk

1 Preheat the oven to moderate 180°C (350°F/ Gas 4). Heat half the oil and half the butter in a large frying pan. Add the meat in batches and cook over medium heat, stirring constantly until well browned; break up any lumps with a fork while cooking. Remove each batch from the pan to a bowl and set aside.

2 Add the remaining oil and butter to the pan. Stir in the onion and carrot, and cook over medium heat for 3–4 minutes or until lightly browned.

3 Return the meat to the pan. Stir in the tomato sauce, stock and undrained tomatoes. Bring to the boil, reduce the heat and simmer for 10–15 minutes or until the liquid reduces and the mixture is thicker.

4 Stir in the peas and cook for 2 minutes. Remove the pan from the heat.

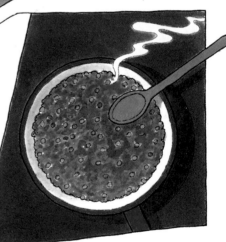

5 Peel and chop the potatoes. Place them in a large pan with enough water to almost cover them. Bring to the boil, reduce the heat and cook for about 5–10 minutes or until soft. The smaller you cut the potato, the faster it will cook.

6 Drain the potato then return it to the pan. Add the extra butter and milk, and mash with a potato masher until smooth and creamy. Season with salt and pepper.

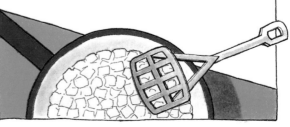

7 Spoon the meat mixture into a 1.5 litre capacity ovenproof dish. Spread the mashed potato over the top with a flat-bladed knife. Place the dish on a baking tray and bake for 20 minutes, or until lightly golden on top. Serve immediately.

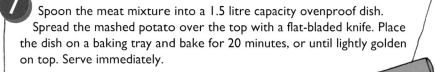

NOTE If using a cut of beef rather than the mince, chop it finely with a large kitchen knife or process it in short bursts in a food processor. Rump or sirloin steak is suitable. Cottage Pie is a great way to use up leftover raw or cooked vegetables. This pie is often made with chopped leftover roast meat. When lamb is used, the name of the dish usually becomes Shepherds Pie.

RISOTTO

Preparation time: 10 minutes
Total cooking time: 30 minutes
Serves 4-6

★★

1 litre chicken stock (page 7)

60 g (2 oz) butter

2 tablespoons olive oil

1 small onion, finely chopped

1¹/₃ cups (295 g/9¹/₂ oz) arborio rice

¹/₂ cup (50 g/1²/₃ oz) freshly grated Parmesan cheese

1 Put the stock into a pan and bring it to the boil. Reduce the heat and keep the stock simmering gently.

2 Combine the butter and oil in another pan and cook the onion over low heat until soft.

3 Add the rice and cook, stirring, for a couple of minutes, or until the rice is well coated with the oil.

4 Add ¹/₂ cup (125 ml/4 fl oz) stock to the rice and stir constantly until all the liquid has been absorbed.

5 Continue adding the stock, ¹/₂ cup at a time, stirring until absorbed between each addition. This is quite time-consuming; don't be tempted to increase the heat or the stock will evaporate rather than be absorbed.

6 When all the stock has been added, the rice should be creamy (but not gluggy) and just cooked.

7 Stir the cheese into the rice until it has melted through.

VEGETARIAN CHILLI

1 Put the burghul in a heatproof bowl and pour in 1 cup (250 ml/8 fl oz) of hot water. Leave to stand until needed.

2 Heat the oil in a large pan and add the onion. Cook for about 10 minutes over medium heat, stirring occasionally, or until soft and lightly golden.

3 Add the garlic, cumin, chilli and cinnamon, and stir-fry for 1 minute.

4 Add all the remaining ingredients and stir to combine. Reduce the heat to low and simmer for 30 minutes.

Preparation time:
15 minutes
Total cooking time:
about 30 minutes
Serves 6

★

3/4 cup (130 g/4 1/4 oz) burghul

2 tablespoons olive oil

1 onion, finely chopped

2 cloves garlic, crushed

2 teaspoons ground cumin

1 teaspoon chilli powder

1/2 teaspoon ground cinnamon

2 x 410 g (13 oz) cans crushed tomatoes

3 cups (750 ml/24 fl oz) vegetable stock (page 7)

440 g (14 oz) can red kidney beans, drained

440 g (14 oz) can chickpeas, drained

315 g (10 oz) can corn kernels, drained

2 tablespoons tomato paste

VEGETABLE PIE

1 Peel the pumpkin and cut it into chunks about 2 cm (³/₄ inch) big. Peel the potato and cut it into chunks of the same size. Roughly chop the broccoli and carrot into similarly sized pieces.

2 Remove the seeds and white membrane from the red pepper and cut it into pieces about 2 cm (³/₄ inch) square.

Preparation time: 40 minutes
Total cooking time:
about 50 minutes
Serves 4

★

200 g (6¹/₂ oz) pumpkin

1 small potato

150 g (4³/₄ oz) broccoli

1 medium carrot

¹/₂ small red pepper (capsicum)

¹/₂ cup (80 g/2²/₃ oz) frozen minted peas

3 spring onions, chopped

80 g (2²/₃ oz) Cheddar cheese, grated

1 clove garlic, crushed, optional

¹/₂ cup (125 ml/4 fl oz) cream

2 eggs

2 sheets ready-rolled puff pastry

sesame seeds

3 Cook the pumpkin, potato, broccoli and carrot by plunging them in batches into a large pan of boiling water. Cook for 1–3 minutes, or until just tender. Remove with a slotted spoon and drain well; cool. (The vegetables can also be cooked in batches in the microwave oven for 2–3 minutes on High (100%), or until just tender.)

4 Preheat the oven to moderately hot 200°C (400°F/Gas 6). Line a baking tray with non-stick baking paper or foil.

5 Combine all the cooked vegetables, red pepper, peas, spring onion and cheese in a large bowl. Whisk the crushed garlic and half the cream together, add some salt and pepper, and then stir the cream mixture into the vegetable mixture.

6 Whisk the remaining cream with the eggs. Lay a sheet of pastry on the prepared tray. Brush the pastry with a little egg mixture. Spoon the vegetable mixture onto the pastry. Pack the vegetables closely together, leaving a border about 4 cm (1¹/₂ inches) wide around the entire edge of the pastry.

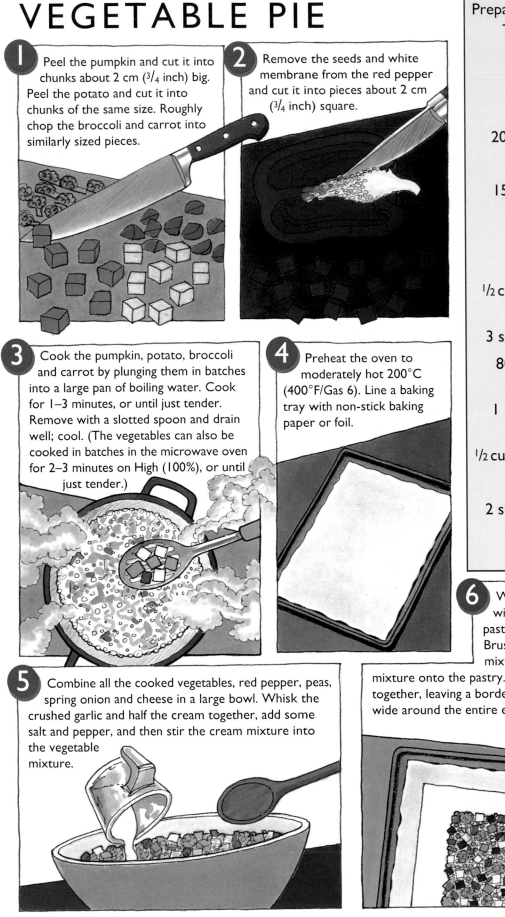

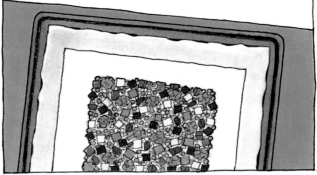

7 Lay the remaining pastry sheet over the top. Press the edges to the base to seal. Fold the border of the bottom pastry sheet over the top and crimp the edges together with a fork. Brush the whole pie with the egg mixture. Cut a cross about 2 cm (³/₄ inch) long in the top of the pie and fold back the points to make a small square. Sprinkle with sesame seeds.

8 Bake for 35–40 minutes, or until puffed and golden. Remove from the oven and carefully pour the remaining egg and cream mixture into the hole on top of the pie. Return the pie to the oven and bake for a further 10 minutes. Allow the pie to stand for 5 minutes before cutting and serving.

STEAK DIANE

1 Trim the excess fat and sinew from each steak. Lay each steak between 2 sheets of plastic wrap and flatten it with a meat mallet or rolling pin until about 1.5 cm (⁵/₈ inch) thick.

2 Remove the plastic, spread the garlic over both sides of each steak and grind over the pepper.

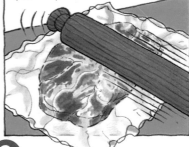

Preparation time: 20 minutes
Total cooking time:
10–12 minutes
Serves 4

★

4 fillet steaks, about 150 g
(4³/₄ oz) each

2 cloves garlic, crushed

freshly ground black pepper

50 g (1²/₃ oz) butter

4 spring onions, finely chopped

2 teaspoons Dijon mustard

2 tablespoons Worcestershire sauce

1 tablespoon brandy

¹/₃ cup (80 ml/2³/₄ fl oz) cream

2 tablespoons finely chopped fresh
parsley

3 Heat half the butter in a frying pan. Cook the steaks over high heat for 1 minute to seal each side, turning only once. Cook a further 1 minute each side for rare steaks, 2 minutes on each side for medium steaks, and 3–4 minutes on each side for well-done steaks. Remove the meat from the pan; cover and keep warm.

4 Heat the remaining butter in the pan; add the spring onion and cook for 1 minute. Add the mustard, Worcestershire sauce and brandy. Stir to dislodge any crusty bits from the base of the pan.

5 Stir in the cream; simmer for about 3–4 minutes, or until reduced slightly. Stir in the parsley. Return the steaks to the pan until just heated through. Serve immediately with the sauce.

CHICKEN CACCIATORE

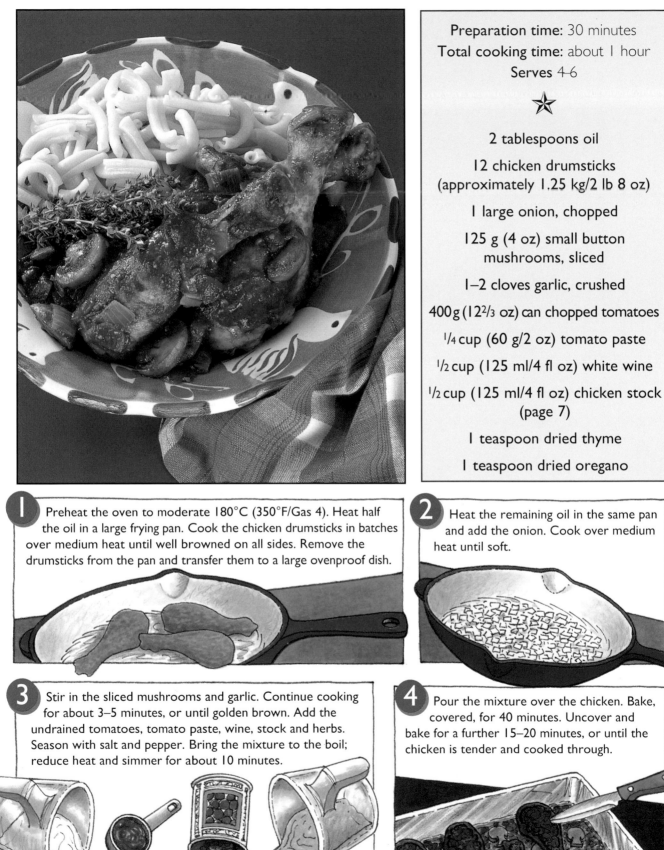

Preparation time: 30 minutes
Total cooking time: about 1 hour
Serves 4-6

★

2 tablespoons oil

12 chicken drumsticks
(approximately 1.25 kg/2 lb 8 oz)

1 large onion, chopped

125 g (4 oz) small button
mushrooms, sliced

1–2 cloves garlic, crushed

400 g (12^{2}/$_{3}$ oz) can chopped tomatoes

^{1}/$_{4}$ cup (60 g/2 oz) tomato paste

^{1}/$_{2}$ cup (125 ml/4 fl oz) white wine

^{1}/$_{2}$ cup (125 ml/4 fl oz) chicken stock
(page 7)

1 teaspoon dried thyme

1 teaspoon dried oregano

1 Preheat the oven to moderate 180°C (350°F/Gas 4). Heat half the oil in a large frying pan. Cook the chicken drumsticks in batches over medium heat until well browned on all sides. Remove the drumsticks from the pan and transfer them to a large ovenproof dish.

2 Heat the remaining oil in the same pan and add the onion. Cook over medium heat until soft.

3 Stir in the sliced mushrooms and garlic. Continue cooking for about 3–5 minutes, or until golden brown. Add the undrained tomatoes, tomato paste, wine, stock and herbs. Season with salt and pepper. Bring the mixture to the boil; reduce heat and simmer for about 10 minutes.

4 Pour the mixture over the chicken. Bake, covered, for 40 minutes. Uncover and bake for a further 15–20 minutes, or until the chicken is tender and cooked through.

TUNA MORNAY

Preparation time: 25 minutes
Total cooking time:
35–40 minutes
Serves 4

⭐

1 1/2 cups (375 ml/12 fl oz) milk

1 bay leaf

5 black peppercorns

425 g (13 1/2 oz) can tuna, in brine

60 g (2 oz) butter

1 onion, chopped

1 celery stick, finely sliced

1/4 cup (30 g/1 oz) plain flour

1/4 teaspoon nutmeg

1/3 cup (80 ml/2 3/4 fl oz) cream

2–3 tablespoons chopped gherkins, optional

1/4 cup (15 g/1/2 oz) chopped fresh parsley

100 g (3 1/3 oz) Cheddar cheese, grated

1/2 cup (40 g/1 1/3 oz) fresh breadcrumbs

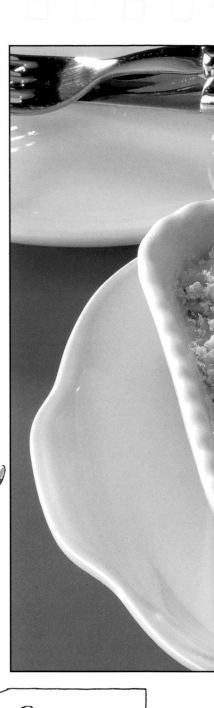

1 Preheat the oven to moderate 180°C (350°F/Gas 4). Place the milk, bay leaf and peppercorns in a medium pan. Slowly bring to the boil, then remove immediately from the heat. Leave to infuse for 15 minutes. Strain and reserve the milk. The milk will now be flavoured by the bay leaf and peppercorns.

2 Drain the can of tuna and reserve the brine. Flake the tuna (i.e. separate the flesh) with a fork.

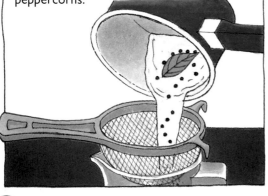

3 Heat the butter in a medium pan. Add the onion and celery, and cook, stirring, for 5 minutes, or until soft. Stir in the flour and cook for 1 minute.

4 Remove the pan from the heat and gradually stir in the milk and reserved tuna brine. Return the pan to the stove; stir the mixture constantly over low heat until it boils and thickens. Simmer gently for 2–3 minutes.

5 Stir in the nutmeg, cream, gherkins, parsley and half the cheese. Remove from heat and stir in the tuna. Season with salt and pepper.

6 Spoon the mixture into a greased 3 cup (750 ml/24 fl oz) capacity ovenproof dish. Sprinkle the remaining cheese and the breadcrumbs over the top. Bake for 15 minutes, or until golden. Serve with rice or pasta.

NOTE

Canned salmon may be used in place of the tuna. For extra flavour, add canned corn kernels or some chopped asparagus spears.

PAN-FRIED FISH WITH LEMON

Preparation time: 10 minutes
Total cooking time:
5 minutes
Serves 4

★

4 large or 8 small fish fillets

20 g (²/₃ oz) butter

a little olive oil

lemon wedges

fresh chopped basil or
lemon thyme

1 Remove any protruding bones from the fish fillets. Trim any excess skin.

2 Heat the butter and a little oil in a large non-stick frying pan. When sizzling, add the fish fillets (you may need to do this in batches). Cook the fish for 2–3 minutes each side, until the flesh flakes when tested with a fork. The cooking time will vary according to the type of fish and the size of the fillets.

3 Squeeze a little lemon juice over each fillet in the pan. Sprinkle with the freshly chopped herbs and some salt and pepper. Serve immediately.

NOTE This recipe is suitable for all types of fish fillets. Each time you make this dish try using a different fish. You will soon discover which ones you prefer. Fish varies in flavour from very mild to oily and strong. Ask your local fishmonger for advice when selecting fish. Remember to rinse your fish under cold water and pat dry with paper towels before cooking.

LAMB CURRY

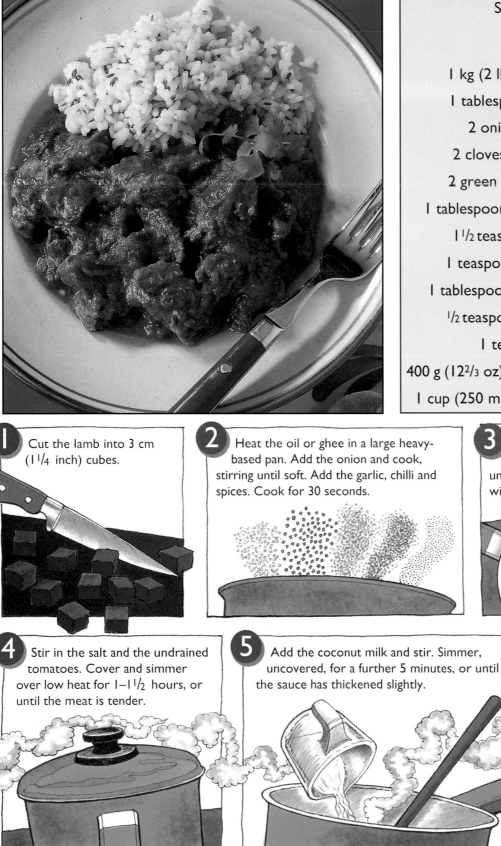

Preparation time: 30 minutes
Total cooking time: 1¼–1¾ hours
Serves 4-6

★

1 kg (2 lb) boneless lamb

1 tablespoon oil or ghee

2 onions, chopped

2 cloves garlic, crushed

2 green chillies, chopped

1 tablespoon grated fresh ginger

1½ teaspoons turmeric

1 teaspoon ground cumin

1 tablespoon ground coriander

½ teaspoon chilli powder

1 teaspoon salt

400 g (12⅔ oz) can chopped tomatoes

1 cup (250 ml/8 fl oz) coconut milk

1 Cut the lamb into 3 cm (1¼ inch) cubes.

2 Heat the oil or ghee in a large heavy-based pan. Add the onion and cook, stirring until soft. Add the garlic, chilli and spices. Cook for 30 seconds.

3 Add the meat and cook, stirring, over high heat until all the meat is well coated with the spice mixture.

4 Stir in the salt and the undrained tomatoes. Cover and simmer over low heat for 1–1½ hours, or until the meat is tender.

5 Add the coconut milk and stir. Simmer, uncovered, for a further 5 minutes, or until the sauce has thickened slightly.

NOTE **A boned leg of lamb is a suitable cut for this recipe. You may use beef if you prefer. Choose a cut that is used for stewing like chuck or skirt.**

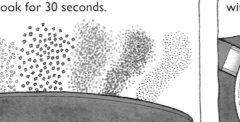

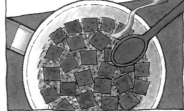

37

ROAST LAMB WITH VEGETABLES

Preparation time: I hour
Total cooking time:
I hour 15 minutes
Serves 4-6

★

1.5 kg (3 lb) leg of lamb

12 large cloves garlic

6 large potatoes, peeled

500 g (1 lb) piece of pumpkin, peeled

I large white or orange sweet potato, peeled

1/4 cup (60 ml/2 fl oz) oil

40 g (1 1/3 oz) butter

Mint Sauce

1/4 cup (60 ml/2 fl oz) water

1/4 cup (60 g/2 oz) sugar

2 tablespoons vinegar

1/4 cup (15 g/1/2 oz) chopped fresh mint

1 Preheat the oven to moderate 180°C (350°F/Gas 4). Trim the lamb of excess fat. Rub a little pepper over the skin. Put the whole garlic cloves in the bottom of a baking dish. Place the meat on a roasting rack and put in the baking dish.

2 Cut the potato, pumpkin and sweet potato in even-sized pieces. Pat them dry with paper towels.

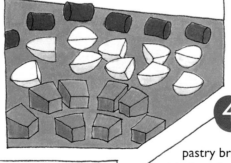

3 Bake the lamb for 1 1/4 hours for a medium-rare result. Meanwhile, heat the oil and butter in another large baking dish in the oven for about 5 minutes, or until hot.

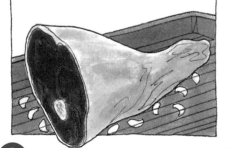

4 Place the vegetables in the dish with the hot butter and oil; use a pastry brush or turn the pieces to coat them with the mixture. Bake for about 50 minutes, or until cooked through and golden, turning once. When cooking the vegetables, time them so they will be ready at the same time as the meat.

5 **To make Mint Sauce:** Combine the water and sugar in a small pan. Stir over low heat until the sugar dissolves. Bring to the boil, reduce the heat and simmer for about 3 minutes. Remove from the heat and stir in the vinegar and mint. Cool slightly and serve in a jug.

6 When the meat is cooked, remove it from the oven and cover with foil. Allow it to rest for 5–10 minutes before carving. Serve slices of meat with the garlic cloves, baked vegetables and Mint Sauce. If you wish to make gravy, see page 9 for the recipe.

CHICKEN WITH CREAMY MUSHROOM SAUCE

Preparation time: 15 minutes
Total cooking time:
25 minutes
Serves 4

30 g (1 oz) butter

4 chicken breast fillets

350 g (11¼ oz) button
mushrooms, sliced

½ cup (125 ml/4 fl oz) chicken
stock (page 7)

½ cup (125 ml/4 fl oz) cream

1 clove garlic, crushed

1 tablespoon chopped fresh
chives

1 Melt the butter in a frying pan and cook the breast fillets 2 at a time over medium heat for 4 minutes each side, or until golden brown.

2 Transfer the chicken to a plate, cover with foil and keep warm.

3 Add the mushrooms to the juices in the pan and cook, stirring occasionally, for 5 minutes, or until soft.

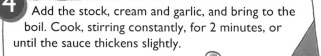

4 Add the stock, cream and garlic, and bring to the boil. Cook, stirring constantly, for 2 minutes, or until the sauce thickens slightly.

5 Stir in the chives and serve the sauce over the chicken breast fillets.

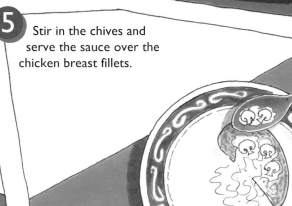

FRIED RICE

Preparation time: 20 minutes
Total cooking time: 10 minutes
Serves 4

★

2 tablespoons oil

2 eggs, lightly beaten

1 onion, cut into thin wedges

250 g (8 oz) sliced ham, chopped

1 1/3 cups (295 g/9 1/2 oz) rice, cooked and completely cooled

1/4 cup (40 g/1 1/3 oz) frozen peas

4 spring onions, chopped

2 tablespoons soy sauce

250 g (8 oz) cooked small prawns, peeled

1 Heat 1 tablespoon of the oil in a large frying pan or wok, and pour in the eggs. Cook the eggs as a flat omelette, turn and cook the other side.

2 Remove the omelette from the pan, cool slightly and chop into small pieces or strips.

3 Heat the remaining oil in the pan, add the onion and stir-fry until it becomes transparent. Add the ham and stir-fry a minute more.

4 Add the rice and peas and stir-fry for about 4 minutes, or until heated through and slightly golden.

5 Stir in the omelette, spring onion, soy sauce and prawns; cook for 1 minute. Serve immediately.

BARBECUE RIBS

Preparation time: 30 minutes
+ marinating
Total cooking time:
about 30 minutes
Serves 4-6

★

1 kg (2 lb) American-style pork
spare ribs

2 cups (500 ml/16 fl oz) tomato
sauce

½ cup (125 ml/4 fl oz) sherry

2 tablespoons Worcestershire
sauce

2 tablespoons soy sauce

2 tablespoons honey

3 cloves garlic, crushed

1 tablespoon grated fresh ginger

1 Using a large sharp knife, cut the racks of ribs into smaller pieces so that each piece has 3 or 4 ribs.

2 Combine the tomato sauce, sherry, Worcestershire sauce, soy sauce, honey, garlic and ginger in a large pan.

3 Add the ribs to the mixture. Bring to the boil; reduce the heat and simmer, covered, for 15 minutes. Rotate the ribs often to ensure even cooking.

4 Transfer the ribs and sauce to a shallow non-metallic dish; allow to cool. Cover with plastic wrap and refrigerate for several hours or overnight.

5 Place the ribs on a preheated, lightly oiled barbecue grill or hotplate. Cook over the hottest part of the fire for 15 minutes, turning and brushing occasionally with any remaining sauce. Serve immediately.

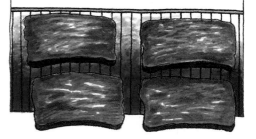

SALMON PATTIES

Preparation time:
25 minutes + 1 hour
refrigeration
Total cooking time:
15 minutes
Serves 4

300 g (9²/₃ oz) potatoes, peeled
and cut into cubes

2 x 200 g (6½ oz) cans red
salmon, drained and with bones
and skin removed

2 spring onions, finely chopped

3 tablespoons chopped parsley

2 teaspoons sweet chilli sauce

1 tablespoon lemon juice

plain flour for dusting

2 eggs, lightly beaten

1 cup (100 g/3¹/₃ oz) dry
breadcrumbs

oil, for shallow-frying

1 Cook the potato in boiling water until it is soft. Drain well, place it in a bowl and mash until smooth.

2 Add the salmon, spring onion, chopped parsley, sweet chilli sauce and lemon juice, and mix to combine.

3 Divide the mixture into 8 equal portions. Shape each portion into round patties with wet hands.

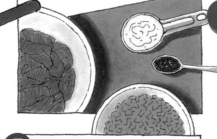

4 Coat the patties lightly with flour, then dip each one into the beaten egg and coat with the breadcrumbs. Cover with plastic wrap and refrigerate for 1 hour.

5 Heat about 1 cm (¹/₂ inch) oil in a frying pan to moderately hot. Add 4 patties to the pan, cook for 4 minutes each side, or until golden brown.

6 Drain the patties on paper towels and keep them warm while you are cooking the remaining patties.

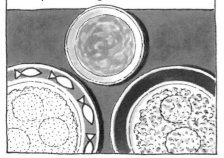

CAFE FOOD AND OTHER SNACKS

NOW YOU DON'T HAVE TO LEAVE THE HOUSE TO INDULGE IN YOUR FAVOURITE CAFE FOOD

BURGER WITH THE WORKS

Preparation time:
25 minutes
Total cooking time:
30 minutes
Serves 4

★

Burgers

500 g (1 lb) lean beef mince

1 onion, finely chopped

1 egg, lightly beaten

$1/3$ cup (25 g/$3/4$ oz) fresh breadcrumbs

2 tablespoons tomato sauce

2 teaspoons Worcestershire sauce

Toppings

30 g (1 oz) butter

2 large onions, cut into rings

4 slices Cheddar cheese

4 rashers bacon

4 eggs

4 large hamburger buns, halved

4 lettuce leaves, shredded

1 large tomato, sliced

4 pineapple rings

tomato sauce

1 Place all the burger ingredients in a mixing bowl. Use your hands to mix together until well combined.

2 Divide the mixture into 4 portions, and shape each portion into a patty.

44

3 Melt the butter in a frying pan and cook the onion rings until soft and golden brown. Set aside and keep warm.

5 In another frying pan cook the bacon (without any butter) until crisp, then fry the eggs—you may need to do them a couple at a time.

4 Cook the burgers in the frying pan for about 4 minutes each side. Place a slice of cheese on each burger, to melt slightly.

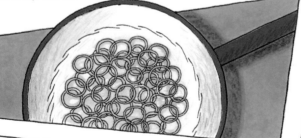

6 Toast the buns under a hot grill for 3–5 minutes and place the bases on serving plates. On each base, place lettuce, tomato and pineapple, then a burger. Follow with onion, bacon, egg, tomato sauce and finally the bun top.

FRENCH TOAST

1 Break the eggs into a wide shallow dish and add the milk and vanilla essence. Beat with a fork or wire whisk until well mixed.

2 Cut the bread slices in half diagonally. Melt half the butter in a frying pan. When the butter begins to bubble, quickly dip a piece of bread into the egg mixture, let the excess run off then place it in the pan.

3 Cook for 1–2 minutes. When the underside is golden, turn the bread over and cook the other side.

4 Transfer the French Toast to a warm plate and cover it with foil. Add more butter to the pan as necessary and cook the remaining bread. Serve sprinkled lightly with cinnamon and sugar. Also delicious with maple syrup.

Preparation time: 10 minutes
Total cooking time:
about 12 minutes
Serves 2

★★

2 eggs

1 cup (250 ml/8 fl oz) milk

1/2 teaspoon vanilla essence

4 thick slices of day-old bread

40 g (1 1/3 oz) butter

cinnamon and sugar, to serve

POLENTA

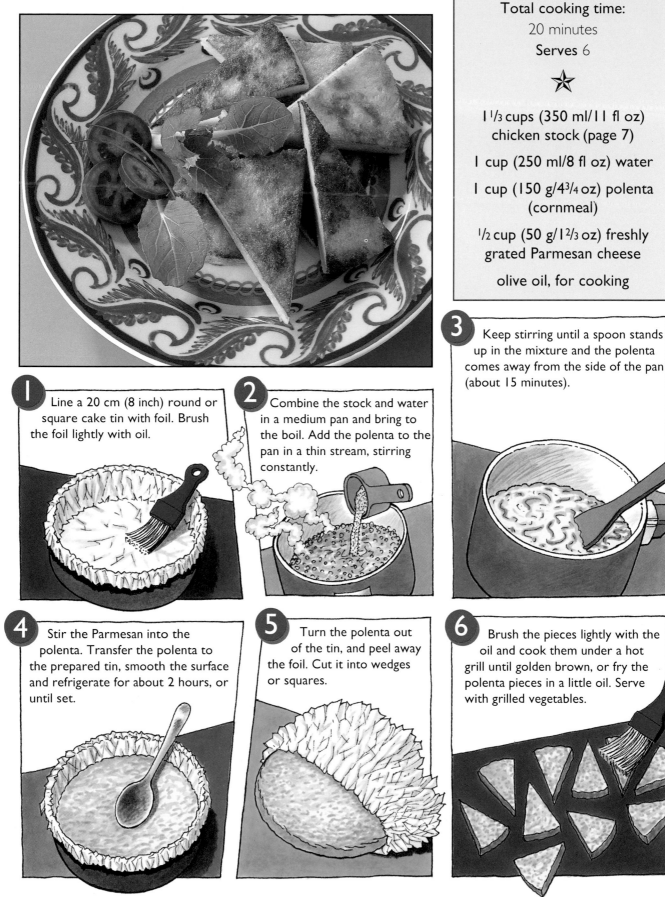

Preparation time: 10 minutes
Total cooking time:
20 minutes
Serves 6

★

1 1/3 cups (350 ml/11 fl oz)
chicken stock (page 7)

1 cup (250 ml/8 fl oz) water

1 cup (150 g/4 3/4 oz) polenta
(cornmeal)

1/2 cup (50 g/1 2/3 oz) freshly
grated Parmesan cheese

olive oil, for cooking

1 Line a 20 cm (8 inch) round or square cake tin with foil. Brush the foil lightly with oil.

2 Combine the stock and water in a medium pan and bring to the boil. Add the polenta to the pan in a thin stream, stirring constantly.

3 Keep stirring until a spoon stands up in the mixture and the polenta comes away from the side of the pan (about 15 minutes).

4 Stir the Parmesan into the polenta. Transfer the polenta to the prepared tin, smooth the surface and refrigerate for about 2 hours, or until set.

5 Turn the polenta out of the tin, and peel away the foil. Cut it into wedges or squares.

6 Brush the pieces lightly with the oil and cook them under a hot grill until golden brown, or fry the polenta pieces in a little oil. Serve with grilled vegetables.

47

HOTCAKES

1 Sift the flour, salt and baking powder into a large mixing bowl. Make a well in the centre.

2 Combine the eggs, milk and vanilla essence in a jug. Beat with a fork until well combined.

Preparation time: 5 minutes
Total cooking time:
about 20 minutes
Makes about 8

★ ★

2 cups (250 g/8 oz) self-raising flour

pinch of salt

1 teaspoon baking powder

3 eggs

1½ cups (375 ml/12 fl oz) milk

½ teaspoon vanilla essence

50 g (1⅔ oz) butter, melted and cooled slightly

butter, for cooking

maple syrup and fruit, to serve

3 Add the milk mixture and the melted butter to the flour, stirring until just combined. The mixture will be slightly lumpy; this is okay. Don't overbeat it or the pancakes will end up tough.

4 Melt about ½ teaspoon of butter in a frying pan over medium heat. Drop ¼ cup (60 ml/ 2 fl oz) of mixture at a time into the pan. It should spread to about a 14 cm (5½ inch) round.

5 Cook until small holes appear in the surface and the underside is golden.

6 Turn the hotcake over and cook a further minute, until it puffs up slightly. Don't flatten the hotcake with the spatula.

7 If you want to serve the hotcakes all together, keep them warm on a plate covered with foil, in a very low oven, while you cook the rest.

NOTE

Hotcakes are delicious served just with whipped butter and maple syrup, or you can top them with sliced banana, strawberries or kiwi fruit or canned fruit as well. As a variation, gently fold some fresh blueberries through the batter just before cooking.

BEAN NACHOS

Preparation time: 10 minutes
Total cooking time: 5 minutes
Serves 4

★

440 g (14 oz) can red kidney beans

1/3 cup (90 g/3 oz) ready-made tomato salsa

250 g (8 oz) corn chips

2 cups (250 g/8 oz) grated Cheddar cheese

1 1/2 cups (375 g/12 oz) ready-made tomato salsa, extra

1 avocado, sliced

1/3 cup (90 g/3 oz) sour cream

1 Preheat the oven to moderate 180°C (350°F/Gas 4). Rinse the kidney beans and drain well. Combine the beans in a small pan with the salsa and stir over medium heat until just heated through.

2 Divide the bean mixture among 4 ovenproof serving plates. Cover with corn chips and grated cheese.

3 Place the dishes in the oven and cook until the cheese has melted.

4 To serve, spoon the extra salsa onto the melted cheese, then top with slices of avocado and a dollop of sour cream. Serve immediately.

GOURMET PIZZAS

Preparation time:
20 minutes
Total cooking time:
25 minutes
Serves 4

3/4 cup (150 g/4³/4 oz)
sun-dried tomatoes in oil

1 clove garlic, crushed

1 tablespoon pine nuts

4 individual pizza bases

1 red (Spanish) onion, thinly
sliced

2 tomatoes, cut into wedges

4 artichoke hearts,
quartered

150 g (4³/4 oz) feta cheese

1 Preheat the oven to hot 210°C (415°F/Gas 6–7). Drain the sun-dried tomatoes, reserving the oil. You will need ¹/4 cup (60 ml/2 fl oz); if there isn't enough, top it up with olive oil.

2 Combine the sun-dried tomatoes, garlic and pine nuts in a food processor and process until well chopped. With the motor running, add the oil in a thin stream to make a smooth paste.

3 Place the pizza bases on a lightly oiled tray. Spread the sun-dried tomato paste onto the bases, and top with the onion, tomato wedges and artichokes.

4 Crumble the feta cheese over the pizzas and bake for 15 minutes, or until the crust is golden brown.

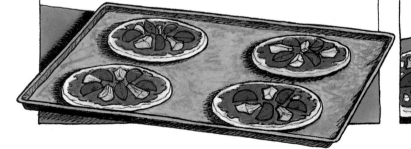

QUICHE LORRAINE

Preparation time: 45 minutes + refrigeration
Total cooking time: 55 minutes
Serves 4

★ ★

1¼ cups (155 g/5 oz) plain flour, sifted

100 g (3⅓ oz) cold butter, chopped

2–3 tablespoons cold water

Filling

3 rashers bacon, finely sliced

60 g (2 oz) Gruyère or Swiss cheese, grated

3 eggs

½ cup (125 ml/4 fl oz) cream

½ cup (125 ml/4 fl oz) milk

a pinch of nutmeg

chopped chives, optional

1 Combine the flour and butter in a large bowl. Using your fingertips, rub the butter into the flour until it resembles breadcrumbs.

2 Stirring with a knife, gradually mix in enough water to combine. Turn the pastry onto a lightly floured work surface and gently press together until smooth.

3 Roll the pastry out between 2 sheets of baking paper large enough to fit into a greased, shallow 23 cm (9 inch) loose-bottomed flan tin.

4 Preheat the oven to moderate 180°C (350°F/Gas 4). Ease the pastry into the tin; trim the edges by rolling a rolling pin across the top of the tin. Refrigerate for 15 minutes.

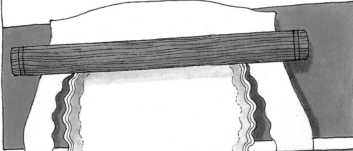

5 Lay a sheet of baking paper over the pastry base. Fill with dried beans or rice. Bake for 10 minutes. Remove the paper and beans or rice. Cook the base for a further 10 minutes. Remove from the oven and cool completely.

6 Cook the bacon in a frying pan over medium heat until crisp. Sprinkle the bacon over the pastry base. Scatter the grated cheese over the top.

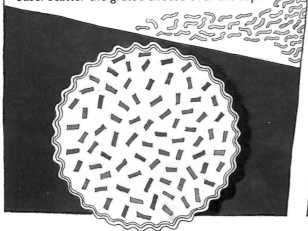

7 Place the flan tin on a baking tray. Whisk the eggs, cream, milk, nutmeg and some pepper in a jug. Pour the egg mixture over the bacon and cheese. Sprinkle with chives, if you wish. Bake the quiche for 30 minutes or until golden and set. Serve hot or cold.

CHICKEN FILLET BURGER

Preparation time: 30 minutes
Total cooking time: 8 minutes
Serves 4

★

4 chicken breast fillets

1/2 cup (60 g/2 oz) plain flour

2 eggs

1 cup (100 g/3 1/3 oz) dry breadcrumbs

2 tablespoons olive oil

1 long breadstick

4 lettuce leaves

1 avocado, sliced

1/3 cup (90 g/3 oz) mayonnaise

1 Trim any excess fat and sinew from the chicken. Flatten each fillet slightly by hitting it with a rolling pin.

2 Spread the flour onto a large plate, lightly beat the eggs in a shallow bowl, and spread the breadcrumbs onto a large plate. Toss the chicken in the flour and shake off excess. Working with 1 fillet at a time, dip it into the egg and then coat it with breadcrumbs, pressing them on firmly. Shake off excess.

3 Heat the oil in a frying pan and cook the chicken for about 4 minutes on each side, or until the chicken is golden brown and cooked through. Drain on paper towels.

4 Cut the breadstick into 4 pieces, and slice horizontally. Toast each side lightly under a hot grill.

5 Place some lettuce and avocado onto each bread base, top with the chicken and a dollop of mayonnaise. Finish with the bread top.

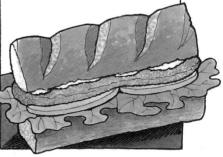

B.L.T.

Preparation time: 15 minutes
Total cooking time: 5 minutes
Serves 2

★

4 rashers bacon

4 slices thick toasting bread

1½ tablespoons mayonnaise

2 large lettuce leaves

1 small tomato

1 Cut the rind from the bacon and cut each rasher in half. Heat a frying pan and add the bacon; cook until crisp and brown. Drain on paper towels.

2 Toast the bread, and spread mayonnaise onto each slice.

3 Shred the lettuce finely, and slice the tomato.

4 Place the lettuce, tomato and bacon onto 2 of the toast slices; top with the other slices.

5 Cut the sandwiches into triangles and serve immediately.

CHICKEN NUGGETS
WITH DIPPING SAUCE

Preparation time: 30 minutes
+ 30 minutes refrigeration
Total cooking time: 30 minutes
Serves 6

★

4 chicken breast fillets

1/2 cup (60 g/2 oz) plain flour

1 tablespoon chicken seasoning

2 eggs

1 1/2 cups (150 g/4 3/4 oz) dry breadcrumbs

oil, for frying

Dipping Sauce

1 cup (250 ml/8 fl oz) pineapple juice

3 tablespoons white wine vinegar

2 teaspoons soy sauce

2 tablespoons soft brown sugar

2 tablespoons tomato sauce

1 tablespoon cornflour

1 tablespoon water

1 Cut the chicken fillets into strips about 2 cm (3/4 inch) wide. Combine the flour and seasoning in a plastic bag and add the chicken strips.

2 Toss the chicken in the bag until evenly coated with flour; remove and shake off excess.

3 Beat the eggs lightly in a shallow bowl, and put the breadcrumbs into a clean plastic bag.

4 Working with a few strips at a time, dip the chicken into the egg, then add to the bag and toss to coat with the breadcrumbs. Transfer to a plate and repeat with the remaining chicken. Refrigerate for at least 30 minutes.

5 Heat 3 cm (1 1/4 inches) oil in a large frying pan to moderately hot. Fry the nuggets in batches for 3–5 minutes, or until golden brown. Drain on paper towels.

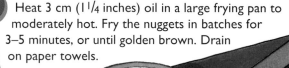

6 To make Dipping Sauce: Combine the juice, vinegar, soy sauce, sugar and tomato sauce in a small pan. Stir constantly over low heat until the sugar has dissolved.

7 Combine the cornflour and water in a small bowl and stir until smooth. Add to the pan and cook, stirring constantly, until the mixture boils and thickens. Reduce the heat and simmer for 2 minutes.

FRITTATA

Preparation time: 20 minutes
Total cooking time: 25 minutes
Serves 6

★

1 kg (2 lb) potatoes

2 tablespoons olive oil

1 large onion, finely chopped

4 eggs

1 Peel the potatoes and cut into 2 cm (³/₄ inch) cubes. Cook in a large pan of boiling water until just tender; drain and cool slightly.

2 Heat the oil in a 25 cm (10 inch) non-stick frying pan. Cook the onion over medium heat until soft and lightly golden.

3 Add the potatoes to the pan, season with plenty of salt and freshly ground black pepper. Cook for about 10 minutes, turning frequently to mix the onion through the potato.

4 Break the eggs into a jug, and beat well with a fork. Pour into the pan, moving the potato so that the egg flows through evenly.

5 Cook for about 5 minutes, or until the egg is set around the edges and base. Preheat the grill to moderately hot.

6 Remove the pan from the stove and place it under the grill until the top of the frittata sets.

7 Place a plate face-down over the pan. Carefully turn the pan over so the frittata comes out onto the plate. Cut into wedges.

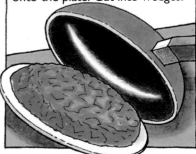

CHICKEN CLUB SANDWICH

Preparation time: 20 minutes
Total cooking time: 10 minutes
Makes 2

★

1/2 BBQ chicken

4 rashers bacon

1/4 cup (60 g/2 oz) mayonnaise

1 tablespoon wholegrain mustard

4 slices rye bread

1/2 avocado, thinly sliced

2 lettuce leaves, shredded

1 tomato, sliced

1 Remove the meat from the chicken bones (including the skin) and cut into shreds.

2 Fry the bacon until crisp and brown. Drain on paper towels.

5 Put the shredded chicken and bacon on next, and season with salt and pepper. Top with the other slices of toast, cut in half diagonally and serve.

4 Toast the bread, and spread 2 slices with the mayonnaise mixture. Top with the avocado, lettuce and tomato.

3 Place the mayonnaise and mustard in a bowl and stir until well combined.

DIPS AND DIPPERS
HUMMUS

1 Place a drained, 410 g (13 oz) can of chickpeas, 2 crushed cloves of garlic, 3 tablespoons of tahini and 3 tablespoons of lemon juice into a food processor and process until finely chopped.

2 With the motor running, gradually add 3 tablespoons of olive oil and process for 1 minute, or until the mixture is smooth. Serve as a dip with vegetable sticks or pitta bread.

GUACAMOLE

1 Cut 2 avocados in half and remove the seeds with the blade of a sharp knife.

2 Peel the avocados and place the flesh into a medium bowl. Mash with a fork until smooth.

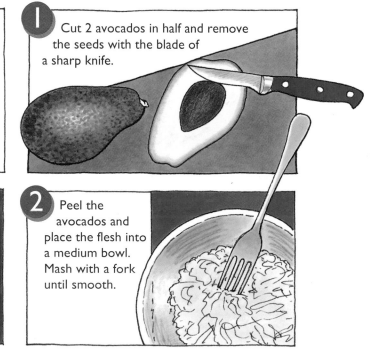

From left: Hummus with chips, crudités and Lavash Dippers; Cream Cheese and Herb Quick Dip, Cucumber and Yoghurt Quick Dip and Guacamole with crudités; French Onion Quick Dip; Corn Relish Quick Dip with Pitta Dippers and Garlic French stick

3 Add 1 finely chopped, small red (Spanish) onion, 1 chopped tomato, 1 tablespoon lemon juice and 3 tablespoons sour cream. Stir to combine. Serve as a dip with vegetable sticks or corn chips.

QUICK DIPS

- Combine 250 g (8 oz) sour cream with a 35 g (1¼ oz) sachet French onion soup mix.
- Finely grate 1 small Lebanese cucumber and squeeze out the excess moisture. Place the grated cucumber, 2 crushed cloves of garlic, 200 g (6½ oz) plain yoghurt and 2 teaspoons chopped mint into a bowl and stir to combine.
- Combine 250 g (8 oz) sour cream with 4 tablespoons corn relish. Mix well.
- Combine 250 g (8 oz) soft cream cheese, 2 tablespoons whole egg mayonnaise, 1 crushed clove of garlic, and 3 tablespoons chopped fresh herbs. Mix well.

DIPPERS

- Split pitta or Lebanese bread in half, brush lightly with oil, sprinkle with grated Parmesan cheese, and cut into triangles. Bake in a preheated moderate 180°C (350°F/Gas 4) oven for 5 minutes, or until crisp and golden.
- Cut lavash bread into large triangles, brush lightly with melted butter and sprinkle with sweet paprika and lemon pepper seasoning. Bake in a preheated moderate 180°C (350°F/Gas 4) oven for 5 minutes, or until crisp and lightly golden.
- Cut carrot, celery, cucumber or pepper (capsicum) into sticks (called crudités).
- Thinly slice 1 French stick, brush lightly with a mixture of olive oil and crushed garlic, and bake in a preheated moderate 180°C (350°F/Gas 4) oven until golden brown.
- Thick 'kettle' style chips make delicious dippers.

SALADS AND VEGETABLES

YOU CAN CHOOSE SIDE DISHES, A FIRST COURSE OR A MAIN DISH FROM THIS HUGE VARIETY OF SALAD AND VEGETABLE DISHES

THOUSAND ISLAND CHICKEN SALAD

Preparation time: 20 minutes
Total cooking time: Nil
Serves 4

★

1 barbecued chicken

1 mignonette lettuce

1 avocado

Dressing

1 cup (250 g/8 oz) mayonnaise

1 tablespoon chilli sauce

1 tablespoon tomato sauce

1/4 cup (45 g/1 1/2 oz) stuffed olives, chopped

1 tablespoon grated onion

2 tablespoons finely chopped red and green pepper (capsicum)

lemon wedges

1 Cut the chicken into serving portions and set aside.

2 Wash the lettuce thoroughly under cold running water. Shake off the excess water. If using large lettuce leaves, tear them into smaller pieces.

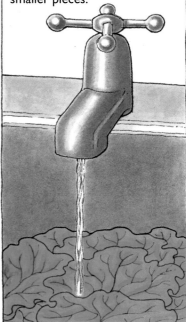

3 Cut the avocado in half, cutting around the stone lengthways. Gently twist both halves in opposite directions to pull them apart.

4 Embed the knife blade in the stone with a sharp tap. Be extremely careful not to slip and cut your hand. Twist the stone out to remove it. Carefully peel away the skin and discard it. Cut the flesh into thin slices.

5 Squeeze a little lemon juice over the avocado to stop it browning. It is usually best to prepare avocados just prior to serving.

6 **To make Dressing:** Combine the mayonnaise, chilli sauce, tomato sauce, olives, onion, red and green pepper in a bowl. Mix until well combined, adding a little milk if the mixture is too thick.

7 Arrange the chicken pieces, salad greens and avocado on individual serving plates. Drizzle with the Dressing. Serve immediately.

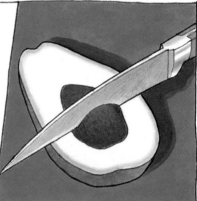

MIXED SALAD

Preparation time: 20 minutes
Total cooking time: Nil
Serves 2–4

★

1 oak leaf lettuce

1 small bunch rocket, optional

1–2 tomatoes

1 Lebanese cucumber

1 small green pepper (capsicum)

2–3 tablespoons fresh chopped chives

Vinaigrette

1/3 cup (80 ml/2³/4 fl oz) olive oil

2–3 tablespoons vinegar or lemon juice

1 teaspoon sugar

1 Wash the lettuce and rocket thoroughly. Gently wrap them in a clean tea towel, hold all the ends of the towel together and shake it to remove the excess water. Tear the leaves into pieces and place them in a large serving bowl.

2 Carefully remove the small core from the top of each tomato. Cut each tomato into about 8 wedges. Slice the cucumber thinly.

3 Cut the green pepper in half lengthways and remove the seeds and white membrane. Cut the flesh into thin strips.

4 Combine the cucumber, tomato, pepper and chives in the bowl with the lettuce and rocket.

5 **To make Vinaigrette:** Whisk the oil, vinegar and sugar together in a small jug. Season with some salt and pepper. Pour the Vinaigrette over the salad just before serving.

GREEK SALAD

Preparation time:
20 minutes
Total cooking time: Nil
Serves 4

★

2 large or 3 small vine-ripened tomatoes

1 green pepper (capsicum)

1 Lebanese cucumber

250 g (8 oz) feta cheese

1 small red (Spanish) onion, thinly sliced, optional

1/3 cup (60 g/2 oz) Kalamata olives

2–3 tablespoons lemon juice

3–4 tablespoons olive oil

1 Carefully remove the small core from the top of each tomato. Cut each tomato into about 8 wedges.

2 Cut the pepper in half and remove the seeds and membrane. Cut the flesh into small squares.

3 Cut the cucumber in half lengthways and then into slices.

4 Cut the feta cheese into small cubes.

5 Combine the tomato, pepper, cucumber, onion (if using), cheese and olives in a large bowl. Drizzle with the lemon juice and oil. Sprinkle with salt and freshly ground black pepper. Stir gently to mix, then serve.

COLESLAW

Preparation time: 20 minutes
Total cooking time: Nil
Serves 4

1/4 small green cabbage

2 medium carrots

2 celery sticks

1 onion, finely chopped

1 small red pepper (capsicum),
finely chopped

Dressing

1/2 cup (125 g/4 oz) mayonnaise

1–2 tablespoons white wine
vinegar

1 teaspoon French mustard

1 Using a large sharp knife, finely shred the cabbage and place it in a large bowl.

2 Grate the carrots on the large side of a grater. Finely chop the celery sticks.

3 Add the onion, red pepper, grated carrot and chopped celery to the cabbage. Toss well to combine.

NOTE **As an alternative, ready-made coleslaw dressings are available in bottles from your local supermarket, some greengrocers and delicatessens.**

4 **To make Dressing:** Whisk together the mayonnaise, vinegar and mustard in a bowl. Season with salt and pepper. Add to the cabbage mixture and toss well to combine. Serve.

POTATO SALAD

Preparation time: 20 minutes
Total cooking time:
about 5 minutes
Serves 4

★

600 g (1¼ lb) potatoes (see note)

1 small onion

2–3 celery sticks, finely chopped

1 small green pepper (capsicum),
chopped

2 tablespoons finely chopped
parsley

Dressing

¾ cup (185 g/6 oz) mayonnaise

1–2 tablespoons vinegar or
lemon juice

2 tablespoons sour cream

1 Wash the potatoes thoroughly and peel them if you prefer. Cut the potatoes into 2 cm (¾ inch) pieces.

2 Cook the potato in a large pan of boiling water for about 5 minutes or until just tender. To test if it is ready, pierce several pieces with a small sharp knife. If the knife comes away easily, the potato is ready. Drain the potato and allow it to cool completely.

3 Peel and finely chop the onion. Combine it in a large bowl with the celery, green pepper and parsley; add the cooled potato.

4 To make Dressing: Mix together the mayonnaise, vinegar or juice and sour cream. Season with salt and pepper to taste. For a thinner dressing, add a little more vinegar or juice.

5 Pour the Dressing over the potato and gently toss to combine, making sure the potato pieces do not break up.

NOTE Any potato is suitable for this recipe. It is not necessary to peel all types of potato; most are delicious with their skins left on.

CAESAR SALAD

Preparation time: 15 minutes
Total cooking time:
10 minutes
Serves 4

★

4 slices white bread

3 rashers bacon, chopped

1 cos lettuce

50 g (1²/₃ oz) shaved Parmesan cheese

Dressing

4 anchovies, chopped

1 egg

2 tablespoons lemon juice

1 clove garlic, crushed

¹/₂ cup (125 ml/4 fl oz) olive oil

1 Preheat the oven to moderately hot 190°C (375°F/Gas 5). Remove the crusts from the bread slices and cut the bread into small cubes.

2 Spread the bread cubes on a baking tray and bake for 10 minutes, or until golden.

3 Fry the bacon pieces until crisp in a pan over medium heat. Drain on paper towels.

4 Tear the lettuce leaves into pieces and put in a salad bowl with the bread cubes, bacon and Parmesan.

5 **To make Dressing:** Put the anchovies, egg, lemon juice and garlic in a food processor or blender. Blend for 20 seconds, or until smooth.

6 With the motor running, add the oil in a thin, steady stream until all the oil is added and the dressing is thick and creamy. Drizzle the dressing over the salad. Season with cracked black pepper.

CORN FRITTERS

Preparation time: 15 minutes
Total cooking time:
3 minutes each batch
Makes 20

★

1¼ cups (155 g/5 oz) plain flour

1½ teaspoons baking powder

½ teaspoon ground coriander

¼ teaspoon ground cumin

130 g (4¼ oz) can corn kernels, drained

130 g (4¼ oz) can creamed corn

½ cup (125 ml/4 fl oz) milk

2 eggs, lightly beaten

2 tablespoons chopped fresh chives

oil, for shallow frying

1 Sift the flour, baking powder, ground coriander and cumin into a medium bowl; make a well in the centre.

2 Add the corn kernels, creamed corn, milk, eggs and chives. Season with salt and pepper and stir until combined.

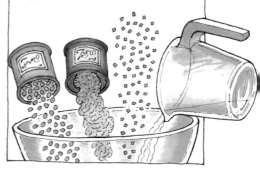

3 Heat the oil in a frying pan. The amount will depend on the size of your pan—the oil should be about 1 cm (½ inch) deep. Drop heaped tablespoons of mixture into the pan, and flatten slightly. Don't overcrowd the pan; cook only a few fritters at a time.

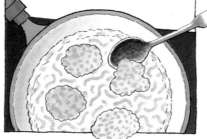

4 Cook each fritter for about 2 minutes, or until the underside is golden. Turn it over and cook for 1 more minute. Drain on paper towels and serve warm.

RATATOUILLE

1 Heat the oil in a large pan and add the onion. Cook over medium heat, stirring occasionally, for about 10 minutes or until very soft and lightly golden brown.

2 Add the garlic and cook for 1 more minute.

3 Meanwhile, cut the eggplants and zucchinis into slices about 2 cm (3/4 inch) thick.

4 Remove the seeds and white membrane from the peppers and cut them into 2 cm (3/4 inch) squares.

5 Add all the vegetables to the pan. Cook, stirring frequently, for about 5 minutes.

6 Reduce the heat to low, cover the pan with a lid and cook for 15 minutes, stirring occasionally.

Preparation time: 20 minutes
Total cooking time: 35 minutes
Serves 6

★

2 tablespoons olive oil

1 large onion, chopped

2 cloves garlic, crushed

3 slender eggplants (aubergines)

3 medium zucchinis (courgettes)

1 green pepper (capsicum)

1 red pepper (capsicum)

3 large tomatoes, chopped

1/3 cup (20 g/2/3 oz) chopped fresh basil

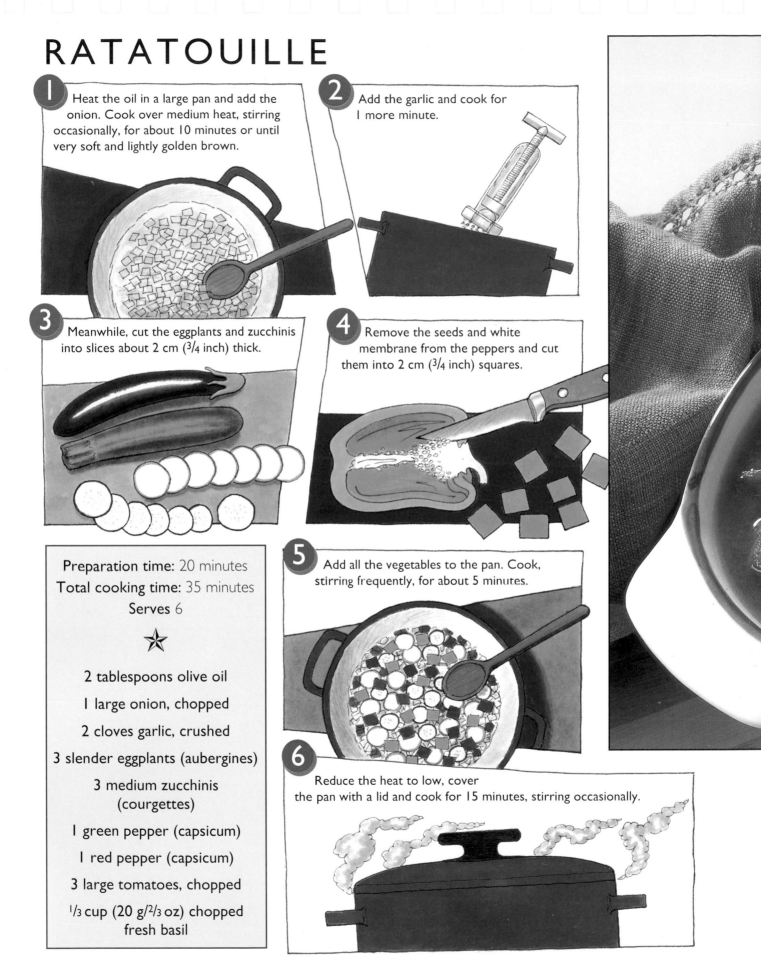

7 Uncover the pan, raise the heat and cook for another 5 minutes to evaporate some of the liquid. Stir in the basil.

NOTE
Ratatouille also makes a great pasta sauce. Or it can be used as a filling for tarts if cooked for a further 30 minutes, until almost dry, and then sprinkled with cheese.

STUFFED MUSHROOMS

Preparation time: 15 minutes
Total cooking time:
25 minutes
Serves 4

★

8 large flat mushrooms

2 tablespoons oil

I small onion, finely chopped

4 rashers bacon, chopped

I cup (80 g/2²/₃ oz) fresh
breadcrumbs

I tablespoon parsley

²/₃ cup (65 g/2¹/₄ oz) grated
Parmesan cheese

1 Preheat the oven to moderate 180°C (350°F/Gas 4) and brush a baking tray with melted butter or oil.

2 To remove the stems of the mushrooms, hold the mushroom in the palm of your hand and twist the stem gently. Finely chop the stems.

3 Heat the oil in a frying pan, add the onion and bacon, and cook until the bacon is lightly browned. Add the chopped mushroom stems and cook for 1 minute.

4 Transfer the mixture to a bowl. Add the breadcrumbs, parsley and grated Parmesan cheese, and stir until combined.

5 Place the mushroom caps onto the prepared baking tray and spoon the filling into the caps. Bake for 20 minutes or until the mushrooms are tender and the topping is golden. Serve immediately.

OVEN FRIES

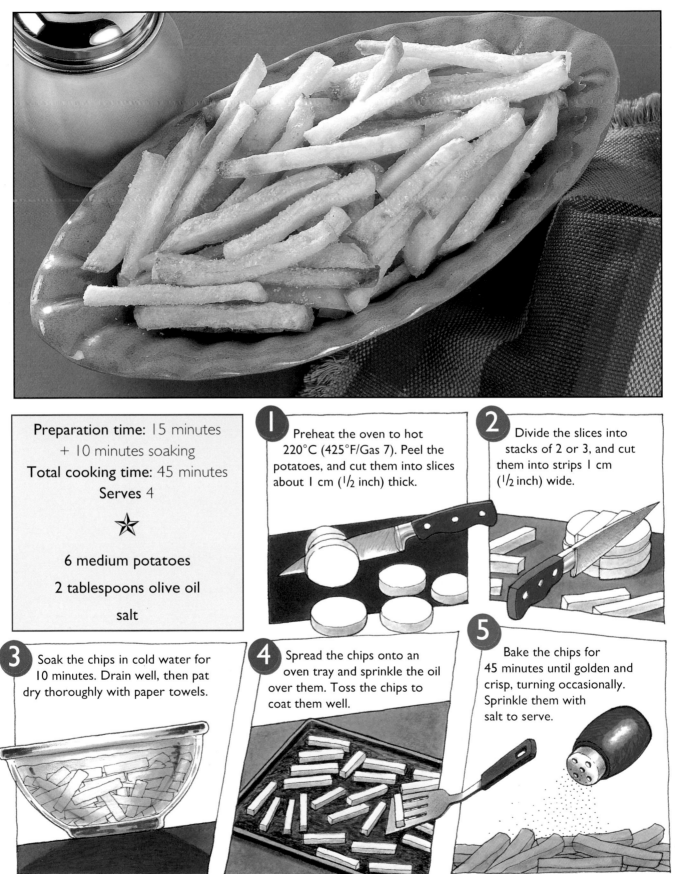

Preparation time: 15 minutes
+ 10 minutes soaking
Total cooking time: 45 minutes
Serves 4

★

6 medium potatoes

2 tablespoons olive oil

salt

1 Preheat the oven to hot 220°C (425°F/Gas 7). Peel the potatoes, and cut them into slices about 1 cm (1/2 inch) thick.

2 Divide the slices into stacks of 2 or 3, and cut them into strips 1 cm (1/2 inch) wide.

3 Soak the chips in cold water for 10 minutes. Drain well, then pat dry thoroughly with paper towels.

4 Spread the chips onto an oven tray and sprinkle the oil over them. Toss the chips to coat them well.

5 Bake the chips for 45 minutes until golden and crisp, turning occasionally. Sprinkle them with salt to serve.

CAULIFLOWER CHEESE

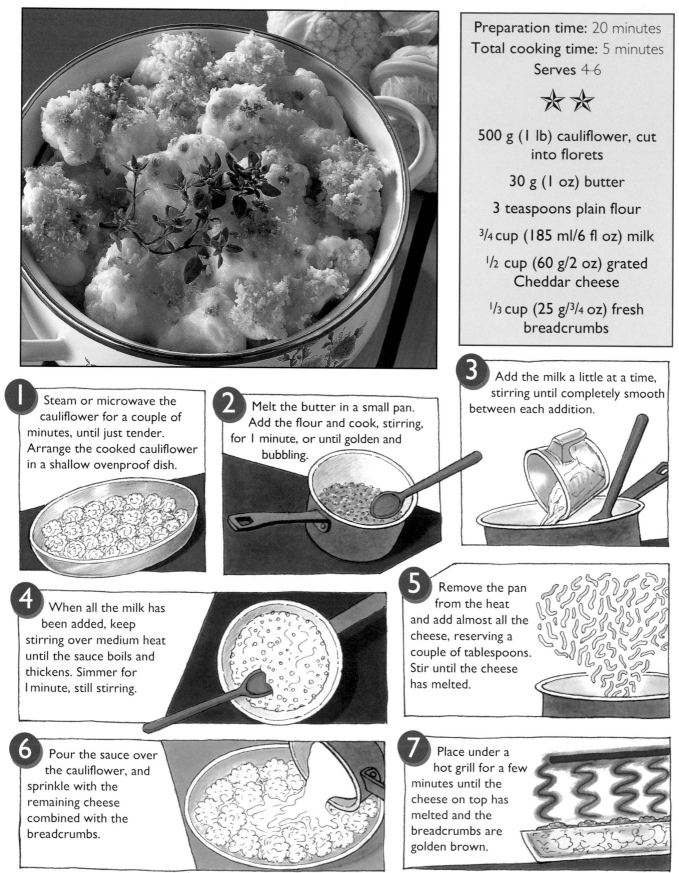

Preparation time: 20 minutes
Total cooking time: 5 minutes
Serves 4-6

★ ★

500 g (1 lb) cauliflower, cut
into florets

30 g (1 oz) butter

3 teaspoons plain flour

3/4 cup (185 ml/6 fl oz) milk

1/2 cup (60 g/2 oz) grated
Cheddar cheese

1/3 cup (25 g/3/4 oz) fresh
breadcrumbs

1 Steam or microwave the
cauliflower for a couple of
minutes, until just tender.
Arrange the cooked cauliflower
in a shallow ovenproof dish.

2 Melt the butter in a small pan.
Add the flour and cook, stirring,
for 1 minute, or until golden and
bubbling.

3 Add the milk a little at a time,
stirring until completely smooth
between each addition.

4 When all the milk has
been added, keep
stirring over medium heat
until the sauce boils and
thickens. Simmer for
1 minute, still stirring.

5 Remove the pan
from the heat
and add almost all the
cheese, reserving a
couple of tablespoons.
Stir until the cheese
has melted.

6 Pour the sauce over
the cauliflower, and
sprinkle with the
remaining cheese
combined with the
breadcrumbs.

7 Place under a
hot grill for a few
minutes until the
cheese on top has
melted and the
breadcrumbs are
golden brown.

SCALLOPED POTATOES

Preparation time: 15 minutes
Total cooking time: 45 minutes
Serves 4

⭐

500 g (1 lb) potatoes

2/3 cup (170 ml/5 1/2 fl oz) milk

1/2 cup (125 ml/4 fl oz) cream

1/2 cup (60 g/2 oz) grated
Cheddar cheese

1/2 teaspoon ground nutmeg

20 g (2/3 oz) butter

1 Brush a 20 cm (8 inch) square shallow ovenproof dish with melted butter or oil, and preheat the oven to moderate 180°C (350°F/Gas 4).

2 Peel the potatoes and cut them into thin slices.

3 Place the slices in layers in the prepared dish, overlapping the slices slightly.

4 Combine the milk and the cream in a jug, and drizzle the mixture over the potatoes.

5 Sprinkle the cheese evenly over the potato, then dust with the nutmeg and dot with butter.

6 Bake for 45 minutes, or until the potato is tender when tested with a knife and the top is golden brown.

VEGETABLES ON THE SIDE

MASHED POTATOES

Peel 4 medium potatoes and cut them into cubes. Cook in a large pan of boiling water for about 5 minutes, or until tender. Drain well. Return the potato to the pan over low heat and mash with a potato masher while any excess liquid evaporates. Add 50 g (1^2/$_3$ oz) butter and ^{1}/$_3$ cup (80 ml/2^3/$_4$ fl oz) milk, and stir in with a fork until light and fluffy. Season with salt and pepper to taste. Serves 4.

HONEY CARROTS

Peel 2 medium carrots and cut them into slices. Steam or boil the carrot for about 3 minutes, or until tender. Drain the carrot well and return it to the pan. Add 30 g (1 oz) butter and 1 tablespoon honey, and toss over medium heat until the butter has melted and the carrot is well coated. Serves 4.

BROCCOLI WITH TOASTED ALMONDS

Cut 400 g (12^2/$_3$ oz) broccoli into florets. Cut a small cross in the base of each floret. Place the broccoli in a steamer, and put it over (or into, depending on the style of your steamer) a pan of boiling water; the water should not touch the vegetables. Cover and steam the broccoli for 2 minutes, or until it is bright green and just tender. Top the broccoli with a dab of butter and sprinkle with lightly toasted slivered almonds. Serves 4.

From left: Honey Carrots; Broccoli with Toasted Almonds; Mashed Potatoes; Asparagus with Parmesan; Glazed Beetroot

ASPARAGUS WITH PARMESAN

Take 155 g (5 oz) of asparagus spears, and gently bend the base of each spear to snap off the woody end. Stand the spears upright in a pan of boiling water for 2 minutes, or until bright green. Use tongs to turn the asparagus over and immerse the tips in the boiling water for 30 seconds. Serve drizzled with a little olive oil and sprinkled with freshly grated Parmesan cheese. Serves 2–4.

GLAZED BEETROOT

Trim the leaves from 1 kg (2 lb) baby beetroot, leaving about 3 cm (1¼ inches) of stalk. Scrub gently under cold water, taking care not to pierce the skin as this causes the beetroot to bleed. Cook whole in boiling water for about 7 minutes, or until tender. Cool slightly, then trim the stalks and tips from the beetroot; cut any larger beetroot in half. The skin should slip off easily. You may want to wear gloves when you do this to prevent your hands and nails from being stained. Return to the pan, and add 30 g (1 oz) butter, 1 tablespoon soft brown sugar, 2 teaspoons fennel seeds and 1 tablespoon malt vinegar. Stir over low heat until the sugar has dissolved and the beetroot are well coated. Serves 4–6.

STUFFED PEPPERS (CAPSICUMS)

Preparation time: 20 minutes
Total cooking time: 45 minutes
Serves 4

2 large red peppers (capsicums)
1/2 cup (110 g/3²/3 oz) short-grain rice
1 tablespoon olive oil
1 onion, finely chopped

2 cloves garlic, crushed
1 tomato, chopped
1 cup (125 g/4 oz) finely grated Cheddar cheese
1/4 cup (25 g/³/4 oz) finely grated Parmesan cheese
1/4 cup (15 g/1/2 oz) chopped basil
1/4 cup (15 g/1/2 oz) chopped parsley

1 Preheat the oven to moderate 180°C (350°F/Gas 4). Cut the peppers in half lengthways, and remove all the seeds and white membrane.

2 Cook the rice in a large pan of boiling water until tender (about 12 minutes). Drain well and set aside in a mixing bowl to cool.

3 Heat the oil in a frying pan and cook the onion for a few minutes until lightly golden. Add the garlic and cook for 1 more minute.

4 Add the onion and garlic to the rice, along with all the remaining ingredients.

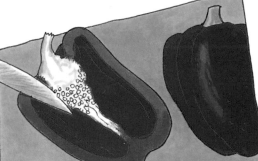

NOTE **Take care to select evenly shaped peppers with flat sides. For a more colourful meal, use a combination of red, green and yellow peppers.**

5 Mix everything together well, and season with salt and freshly ground black pepper to taste.

6 Spoon the rice mixture into the pepper shells, and place them on an oven tray.

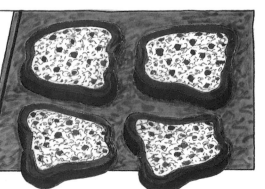

7 Bake for 30 minutes, or until the peppers are soft and the filling is brown on top.

STIR-FRIED CHINESE VEGETABLES

Preparation time: 15 minutes
Total cooking time:
7 minutes
Serves 4

300 g (9²/₃ oz) baby bok choy

100 g (3¹/₃ oz) snake beans

2 spring onions

150 g (4³/₄ oz) broccoli

1 medium red pepper
(capsicum)

2 tablespoons oil

2 cloves garlic, crushed

2 teaspoons grated ginger

1 tablespoon sesame oil

2 teaspoons soy sauce

1 Wash the bok choy and trim away the thick stalks. Cut the leaves into wide strips.

2 Cut the snake beans into 5 cm (2 inch) lengths, and slice the spring onions diagonally. Cut the broccoli into small florets and the red pepper into strips.

3 Heat the oil in a large frying pan or wok. Add the garlic and ginger and cook over medium heat for 30 seconds, stirring constantly.

4 Add the beans, spring onion and broccoli, and stir-fry for 3 minutes.

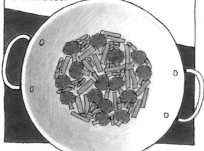

5 Add the pepper, stir-fry for 2 more minutes, then add the bok choy and stir 1 minute more.

6 Stir in the sesame oil and soy sauce, and toss through. Serve immediately.

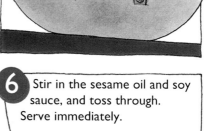

HASH BROWNS

Preparation time: 10 minutes
Total cooking time: 20 minutes
Serves 4

★

2 medium potatoes
salt and pepper
oil, for frying

1 Fill a medium pan with water, and bring to the boil. Peel the potatoes and cut them in half.

2 Put the potatoes into the pan. Bring the water back to the boil, then boil for 10 minutes, or until just tender when pierced with a knife. Don't overcook or the potato will go mushy.

3 Drain the potatoes, and leave until cool enough to handle. Grate the potatoes, place into a bowl and season with salt and pepper; mix through.

4 Shape the grated potato roughly into patties about 10 cm (4 inches) round. The starchiness of the potato will hold the patties together.

5 Heat enough oil to cover the bottom of a frying pan, and cook the patties for a few minutes on each side, or until golden brown and crispy. Drain on paper towels.

SWEET TREATS

EATEN ALL YOUR GREENS? IN THAT CASE, YOU CAN INDULGE YOURSELF IN ONE (OR LOTS!) OF THESE SCRUMPTIOUS GOODIES

FRESH FRUIT PAVLOVA

Preparation time: 20 minutes
Total cooking time:
40 minutes
Serves 6–8

★ ★

4 egg whites

1 cup (250 g/8 oz) caster sugar

1½ cups (375 ml/12 fl oz) cream

1 banana

250 g (8 oz) strawberries

2 kiwi fruit

pulp from 2 passionfruit

1 Preheat the oven to slow 150°C (300°F/Gas 2). Line a baking tray with baking paper. Draw a 20 cm (8 inch) circle on the paper.

2 Using electric beaters, beat the egg whites in a large dry bowl until soft peaks form. Gradually add the sugar, beating well after each addition. Continue beating until the mixture is thick and glossy and the sugar has completely dissolved.

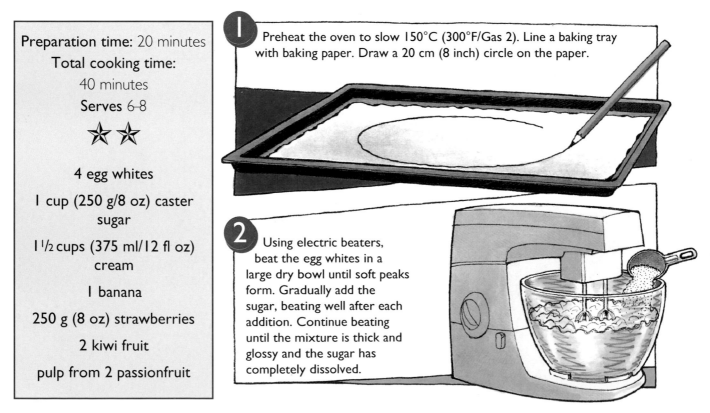

3 To test if the sugar has dissolved, rub a small amount of the mixture between your thumb and forefinger. The mixture should feel just slightly gritty. If it feels very gritty, continue beating for a few minutes more.

5 Shape the meringue by running a palette or flat-bladed knife up and down the edge of the meringue, making furrows around the side. This will strengthen the sides, stopping them from collapsing, and it gives a professional finish. Bake for 40 minutes. Turn the oven off and allow the meringue to cool completely in the oven.

4 Spread the meringue mixture onto the tray inside the marked circle.

6 Whip the cream until soft peaks form. Peel and slice the banana. Halve the strawberries and peel and slice the kiwi fruit. Decorate the pavlova with cream and fresh fruit. Spoon the passionfruit pulp over the top and serve immediately.

NOTE To make individual pavlovas, shape the meringue into 6 cm (2¹/₂ inch) rounds, and bake for 10–15 minutes.

LEMON CHEESECAKE

1 Brush a deep, 20 cm (8 inch) round springform tin with melted butter or oil. Line the base with non-sticking baking paper.

2 Put the biscuits in a food processor and process until finely crushed. Add the spice and melted butter, and process briefly to combine.

3 Press half the crumb mixture into the base of the prepared tin.

4 Gradually press the remainder around the sides of the tin. Use a flat-bottomed glass to press the crumbs firmly into place. Refrigerate while making the filling.

Preparation time:
40 minutes + overnight refrigeration
Total cooking time: Nil
Serves 6–8

250 g (8 oz) honey snap or granita biscuits

1 ½ teaspoons mixed spice

125 g (4 oz) butter, melted

Filling

375 g (12 oz) cream cheese

1 tablespoon grated lemon rind

2 teaspoons vanilla essence

400 g (12²/₃ oz) can sweetened condensed milk

¹/₃ cup (80 ml/2³/₄ fl oz) fresh lemon juice

5 **To make Filling:** Beat the cream cheese with electric beaters until smooth and creamy. Add the lemon rind and vanilla essence. Mix well.

6 Gradually beat in the condensed milk and lemon juice. Beat for 5 minutes, or until the mixture is smooth and slightly thickened.

7 Pour the Filling onto the biscuit base and smooth the surface. Refrigerate the cheesecake overnight. Top the cheesecake with freshly whipped cream sprinkled with nutmeg, and Candied Lemon Slices, if you like (see note).

NOTE

To make Candied Lemon Slices: Place 1 cup (250 g/8 oz) sugar and $^1/_3$ cup (80 ml/2$^3/_4$ fl oz) water in a pan. Stir over low heat without boiling until the sugar dissolves. Bring to the boil and reduce heat. Add 1–2 thinly sliced lemons in batches. Cook each batch for about 5–10 minutes, or until transparent; drain.

STICKY DATE PUDDING

Preparation time:
30 minutes
Total cooking time:
40 minutes
Serves 6-8

★

¹/₂ cup (45 g/1¹/₂ oz)
dessicated coconut

¹/₂ cup (115 g/3³/₄ oz)
firmly packed soft brown
sugar

³/₄ cup (90 g/3 oz)
self-raising flour

¹/₄ cup (30 g/1 oz) plain
flour

¹/₂ teaspoon bicarbonate
of soda

100 g (3¹/₃ oz) butter

¹/₄ cup (90 g/3 oz)
golden syrup

1 cup (185 g/6 oz)
chopped dates

¹/₄ cup (60 ml/2 fl oz)
orange juice

2 eggs, lightly
beaten

Sauce

80 g (2²/₃ oz)
butter

¹/₄ cup (55 g/1³/₄ oz)
firmly packed soft brown
sugar

1 cup (250 ml/8 fl oz)
cream

2 tablespoons golden
syrup

1 Preheat the oven to moderate 180°C (350°F/Gas 4). Brush a deep 20 cm (8 inch) square cake tin with melted butter or oil. Line the base and sides with baking paper.

2 Combine 2 tablespoons each of the coconut and brown sugar and sprinkle over the base of the tin.

3 Sift the flours and soda into a large mixing bowl. Add the remaining coconut and make a well in the centre.

4 Combine the remaining sugar, butter, golden syrup, dates and juice in a pan. Stir over medium heat until the butter melts and the sugar dissolves. Remove from the heat.

5 Using a large metal spoon, fold the date mixture into the dry ingredients. Add the eggs and stir until the mixture is smooth.

6 Pour the mixture into the tin and bake for 35 minutes or until a skewer comes out clean when inserted in the centre. Leave the pudding in the tin for 5 minutes before turning out.

NOTE **Use fresh or dried dates in this recipe.**

7 **To make Sauce:** Combine all the ingredients in a small pan. Stir over low heat until the sugar and butter have dissolved and the mixture is smooth. Stir for a further 2 minutes then serve immediately over slices of the hot pudding. Sprinkle over a little icing sugar and serve with scoops of vanilla ice cream.

APPLE PIE

Preparation time: 1 hour
+ refrigeration
Total cooking time:
about 55 minutes
Serves 4-6

★ ★

1 cup (125 g/4 oz) self-raising flour

1 cup (125 g/4 oz) plain flour

2 tablespoons custard powder,
optional

2 tablespoons caster sugar

155 g (5 oz) cold butter, chopped

1 egg, lightly beaten

3–4 tablespoons iced water

Filling

8 large apples (4 red + 4 green)

4 thick strips lemon rind

1 cinnamon stick

8 whole cloves

1 3/4 cups (440 ml/14 fl oz) water

1/3 cup (90 g/3 oz) caster sugar

1 Sift the flours, custard powder and sugar into a large bowl. Add the butter. Use your fingertips to rub the butter into the flour mixture. Continue rubbing until the mixture resembles breadcrumbs.

2 Make a well in the centre. Using a knife, stir in the egg and enough iced water to mix until the dough just comes together.

3 Turn onto a lightly floured surface and gently press together to form a ball. Wrap in plastic wrap and refrigerate for about 20 minutes.

4 **To make Filling:** Peel, core and cut the apples into large chunks. Combine in a large pan with the rind, cinnamon stick, cloves, water and sugar. Cover and simmer gently for 10 minutes, or until the apples are tender but still firm. Remove from the heat, drain well and discard the rind, cinnamon and cloves. Cool.

5 Preheat the oven to moderate 180°C (350°F/Gas 4). Roll two-thirds of the dough between 2 sheets of baking paper, large enough to cover the base and sides of a greased 23 cm (9 inch) pie plate. Ease the pastry into the plate. Refrigerate for 10 minutes.

6 Roll the remaining pastry between 2 sheets of baking paper, until large enough to cover the top. Spoon the apple into the pie case.

7 Brush the edges with a little beaten egg and milk. Carefully lay the pastry over the top, pressing to seal the edges. Use a small, sharp knife to trim the pastry edges. Pinch, crimp or fork the edges.

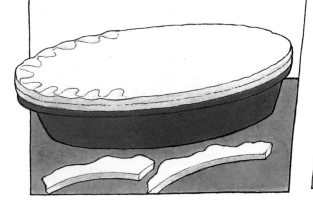

8 Use the remaining pastry scraps to decorate the top. Brush with the egg and milk. Make several slits in the pie top for steam holes. Bake for 45 minutes or until golden and cooked through. Dust the top with icing sugar and serve with custard, cream or ice cream.

LEMON DELICIOUS

Preparation time:
25 minutes
Total cooking time: 1 hour
Serves 4

★ ★

60 g (2 oz) butter

³/₄ cup (185 g/6 oz) caster
sugar

3 eggs, separated

1 teaspoon grated
lemon rind

¹/₃ cup (40 g/1 ¹/₃ oz)
self-raising flour

¹/₄ cup (60 ml/2 fl oz) lemon
juice

³/₄ cup (185 ml/6 fl oz) milk

1 Preheat the oven to moderate 180°C (350°F/Gas 4). Brush a 4 cup (1 litre) capacity ovenproof dish with melted butter.

2 Using electric beaters, beat the butter, sugar, egg yolks and rind in a small bowl until the mixture is light and creamy. Transfer to a medium bowl.

3 Sift the flour into the bowl and stir with a wooden spoon until just combined. Add the juice and milk and stir to combine.

4 Place egg whites in a small, dry bowl and beat with electric beaters until firm peaks form.

5 Use a large metal spoon to fold the egg whites into the flour mixture. Fold until just combined.

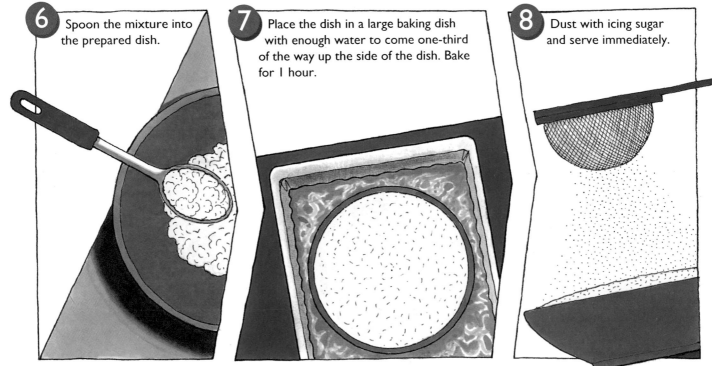

6 Spoon the mixture into the prepared dish.

7 Place the dish in a large baking dish with enough water to come one-third of the way up the side of the dish. Bake for 1 hour.

8 Dust with icing sugar and serve immediately.

GOURMET CARROT CAKE

Preparation time:
40 minutes

Total cooking time: 1 hour
30 minutes

Makes 1 round cake

★

1 cup (125 g/4 oz) self-raising flour

1 cup (125 g/4 oz) plain flour

2 teaspoons ground cinnamon

1/2 teaspoon ground cloves

1 teaspoon ground ginger

1/2 teaspoon ground nutmeg

1 teaspoon bicarbonate of soda

1 cup (250 ml/8 fl oz) oil

1 cup (185 g/6 oz) lightly packed soft brown sugar

4 eggs

1/2 cup (175 g/5^2/3 oz) golden syrup

2 1/2 cups (390 g/12 1/2 oz) grated carrot

1/2 cup (60 g/2 oz) chopped pecans or walnuts

Icing

175 g (5^2/3 oz) cream cheese

60 g (2 oz) butter

1 1/2 cups (185 g/6 oz) icing sugar

1 teaspoon vanilla essence

1–2 teaspoons lemon juice

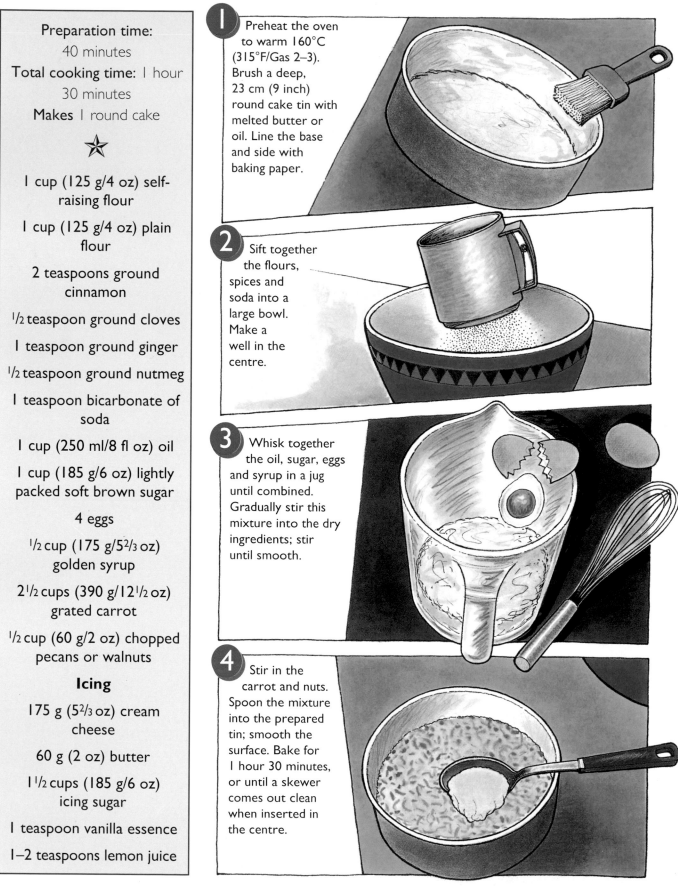

1. Preheat the oven to warm 160°C (315°F/Gas 2–3). Brush a deep, 23 cm (9 inch) round cake tin with melted butter or oil. Line the base and side with baking paper.

2. Sift together the flours, spices and soda into a large bowl. Make a well in the centre.

3. Whisk together the oil, sugar, eggs and syrup in a jug until combined. Gradually stir this mixture into the dry ingredients; stir until smooth.

4. Stir in the carrot and nuts. Spoon the mixture into the prepared tin; smooth the surface. Bake for 1 hour 30 minutes, or until a skewer comes out clean when inserted in the centre.

5 Leave the cake in the tin for at least 15 minutes before turning onto a wire rack to cool.

6 **To make Icing:** Beat the cream cheese and butter with electric beaters until smooth. Gradually add the icing sugar alternately with the vanilla and juice, beating until light and creamy. Spread the Icing over the cooled cake.

NOTE The cake can be cut in half horizontally. Sandwich the layers together with half the Icing and spread the remainder on the top.

MUFFINS

Preparation time:
15 minutes
Total cooking time:
25 minutes
Makes 12

★

2^1/$_2$ cups (310 g/9^3/$_4$ oz)
self-raising flour

^{1}/$_4$ cup (60 g/2 oz) caster
sugar

2 teaspoons baking
powder

2 eggs

1^1/$_2$ cups (375 ml/12 fl oz)
milk or buttermilk

160 g (5^1/$_4$ oz) butter,
melted

1 Preheat the oven to moderately hot 190°C (375°F/Gas 5). Brush a 12-hole muffin tin with melted butter or oil.

2 Sift the flour, sugar and baking powder into a bowl. Make a well in the centre.

3 Add the combined beaten eggs, milk and butter. Stir with a wooden spoon until almost smooth. The ingredients should all be moistened.
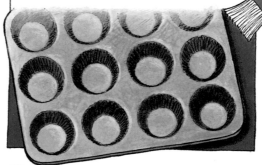

4 Spoon the mixture evenly into the tins. (If you only have a 6-hole tin, you can cook the muffins in 2 batches.)

From left: Banana Muffins; Chocolate Chip Muffins, Blueberry Muffins, basic Muffins; Strawberry Muffins

5 Bake for 20–25 minutes, or until golden brown. To test the muffins, insert a skewer in the centre. It should come out clean if they are ready. Loosen the muffins from the tins and cool on a wire rack.

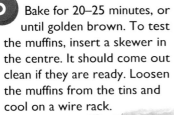

NOTE Add about 155 g (5 oz) of fresh berries to the basic muffin mixture. Choose from blueberries, raspberries, loganberries or boysenberries.

BANANA MUFFINS

1 Use the basic muffin recipe but replace the caster sugar with raw sugar and decrease the butter to 100 g (3¹/₃ oz). Add 2 teaspoons ground cinnamon, 1 cup (240 g/ 8¹/₂ oz) mashed banana and 3 teaspoons grated orange rind when adding the liquid. These muffins can also be made using half wholemeal flour and half white flour.

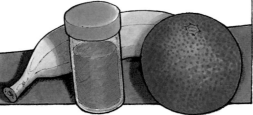

CHOCOLATE CHIP MUFFINS

1 Use the basic muffin recipe and sift 2 tablespoons cocoa powder in with the flour. Add 250 g (8 oz) chopped chocolate or choc bits after the egg mixture. Use either dark, milk or white chocolate or a combination of all 3. Makes 12.

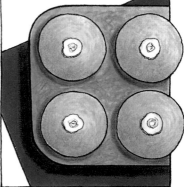

2 Spoon the mixture into the tins and top with a dried banana chip if you like. Bake for 20–25 minutes. Makes 12.

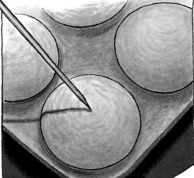

GINGERBREAD PEOPLE

Preparation time: 1 hour
Total cooking time: about
30 minutes
Makes about 16

★ ★

125 g (4 oz) butter

1/2 cup (95 g/3 1/4 oz) lightly packed
soft brown sugar

1/3 cup (115 g/3 3/4 oz) golden syrup

1 egg

2 cups (250 g/8 oz) plain flour

1/3 cup (40 g/1 1/3 oz) self-raising flour

1 tablespoon ground ginger

1 teaspoon bicarbonate of soda

Icing

1 egg white

1/2 teaspoon lemon juice

1 cup (125 g/4 oz) pure icing sugar

food colourings

1 Line 2 or 3 oven trays with baking paper. Using electric beaters, beat the butter, sugar and syrup in a bowl until light and creamy. Add the egg and beat well.

2 Transfer the mixture to a large bowl. Sift in the flours, ginger and soda. Use a knife to mix until just combined.

3 Use a well-floured hand to gather the dough into a ball. Knead gently on a well-floured surface until smooth. Don't over-handle the dough or it will become tough.

4 Lay a sheet of baking paper over a large chopping board. Roll out the dough on the lined board to a 5 mm (1/4 inch) thickness. Preheat the oven to moderate 180°C (350°F/Gas 4).

5 Refrigerate the dough on the board for 15 minutes, or until it is firm enough to cut. Cut the dough into shapes using assorted gingerbread people cutters. Press any remaining dough together. Re-roll and cut out into shapes.

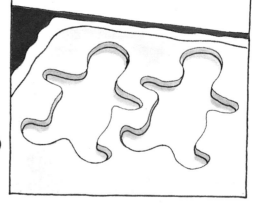

6 Bake for 10 minutes or until lightly browned. Cool the biscuits on the trays, then decorate with the icing.

7 **To make Icing:** Beat the egg white in a small bowl with electric beaters until soft peaks form. Gradually add the lemon juice and sifted icing sugar; and beat until thick and creamy.

8 Divide the icing into several bowls and tint with food colourings.

9 Spoon into small paper icing bags (see page 7) and use to decorate the biscuits.

ULTIMATE CHOCOLATE BROWNIES

Preparation time:
20 minutes
Total cooking time:
45 minutes
Makes about 30

★

1/3 cup (40 g/1 1/3 oz)
plain flour

1/2 cup (60 g/2 oz)
dark cocoa powder

2 cups (500 g/1 lb) sugar

1 cup (125 g/4 oz) chopped
pecans or pistachios

250 g (8 oz) dark chocolate

250 g (8 oz) butter

2 teaspoons vanilla essence

4 eggs, lightly beaten

1 Preheat the oven to moderate 180°C (350°F/Gas 4). Brush a 20 x 30 cm (8 x 12 inch) rectangular cake tin with melted butter or oil. Line the base and sides with baking paper.

2 Sift the flour and cocoa into a large bowl, add the sugar and nuts and mix well.

3 Use a large sharp knife to chop the chocolate into small pieces. Stir it into the sugar mixture and make a well in the centre.

4 Melt the butter in the microwave oven or in a small pan over low heat.

5 Pour the butter, vanilla and beaten eggs onto the dry ingredients. Stir until all ingredients are moistened and combined.

6 Pour the mixture into the tin; smooth the surface. Bake for 45 minutes. Cool it in the tin before cutting it into squares.

COCONUT MACAROONS

Preparation time: 15 minutes
Total cooking time:
15–20 minutes
Makes about 40

★★

3 egg whites

1¼ cups (310 g/9¾ oz) caster sugar

½ teaspoon coconut essence

2 tablespoons cornflour, sifted

3 cups (270 g/8¾ oz) desiccated coconut

1 Preheat the oven to warm 160°C (315°F/Gas 2–3). Line 2 baking trays with baking paper.

2 Place the egg whites into a small, clean, dry mixing bowl. Beat the egg whites with electric beaters until stiff peaks form.

3 Add the sugar gradually, beating constantly until the mixture is thick and glossy and all the sugar has dissolved.

4 Transfer the mixture to a large mixing bowl and fold in the coconut essence, cornflour and coconut with a large metal spoon.

5 Drop tablespoons of the mixture onto the lined baking trays, about 5 cm (2 inches) apart. Bake for 15–20 minutes, or until the macaroons are lightly golden. Allow the macaroons to cool on the tray before serving.

NOTE The macaroons will keep in an airtight container for up to 2 days.

THE ULTIMATE CHOC-CHIP COOKIE

Preparation time:
30 minutes

Total cooking time:
15 minutes

Makes about 25

★

1 1/2 cups (185 g/6 oz) plain flour

3/4 cup (90 g/3 oz) cocoa powder

1 1/2 cups (280 g/9 oz) lightly packed soft brown sugar

180 g (5 3/4 oz) butter

150 g (4 3/4 oz) dark chocolate, chopped

3 eggs, lightly beaten

1 cup (175 g/5 2/3 oz) dark choc bits

1/3 cup (60 g/2 oz) white choc bits

150 g (4 3/4 oz) nuts of your choice, chopped (see note)

1 Preheat the oven to moderate 180°C (350°F/Gas 4). Line 2 baking trays with non-stick baking paper.

2 Sift the flour and cocoa into a large bowl, and stir in the sugar. Make a well in the centre.

3 Place the butter and chocolate in a medium pan; stir over low heat until the mixture is smooth.

4 Stir the butter mixture and eggs into the dry ingredients. Mix until well combined.

5 Stir in the dark and white choc bits and the nuts.

6 Drop heaped tablespoons of the mixture onto the prepared trays. Be sure to leave room for spreading. Flatten each one slightly with your fingertips.

7 Bake for 15 minutes. Leave the biscuits on the trays for at least 5 minutes before transferring them to a wire rack to cool.

NOTE Use your favourite nuts in this recipe. Choose from macadamias, pecans, almonds, Brazils, walnuts or pistachios. If you prefer, use milk choc bits in place of the dark variety. Chopped chocolate is a good substitute if you don't have any choc bits.

SCONES

Preparation time: 20 minutes
Total cooking time: 12 minutes
Makes 12

★

2 cups (250 g/8 oz) self-raising flour

pinch of salt

30 g (1 oz) butter, chopped

3/4 cup (185 ml/6 fl oz) milk or
buttermilk

extra milk, for glazing

1 Preheat the oven to hot 210°C (415°F/Gas 6–7). Brush a baking tray with melted butter or oil.

2 Sift the flour and salt into a large bowl. Add the butter and rub it in lightly using your fingertips until it looks like fine breadcrumbs.

4 Turn the dough onto a lightly floured surface; knead it briefly and lightly until smooth. Press or roll out the dough until it is 1–2 cm (1/2–3/4 inch) thick. Cut the dough into rounds using a 5 cm (2 inch) cutter.

3 Make a well in the centre. Add almost all the milk or buttermilk. Mix with a flat-bladed knife to a soft dough, adding more liquid if necessary.

From left: Fruit Scones; basic Scones; Spiced Scrolls

5 Place the rounds close together on the prepared tray. Brush the tops with a little milk. Bake for 10–15 minutes, or until golden brown. Serve with butter or whipped cream and jam.

FRUIT SCONES

Use the dough for the Basic Scones and add about 1/3 cup (40 g/11/3 oz) raisins, currants or sultanas to the flour after rubbing in the butter. Mix well, then add the liquid.

SPICED SCROLLS

1 Prepare dough as for Basic Scones. Roll out to a 25 x 40 cm (10 x 16 inch) rectangle.

2 Beat 60 g (2 oz) butter, 2 tablespoons soft brown sugar and 1 teaspoon mixed spice in a small bowl with electric beaters until light and creamy.

3 Spread this mixture over the dough and sprinkle with about 60 g (2 oz) chopped walnuts or pecans. Roll up from the long side.

4 Use a sharp knife to cut into 3 cm (11/4 inch) slices. Lay the slices close together cut-side-up on the tray. Bake for 12 minutes, or until golden. Cool slightly then serve.

CARAMEL SLICE

Preparation time: 40 minutes
Total cooking time:
about 50 minutes
Makes 18–20 pieces

★ ★

1/2 cup (60 g/2 oz) plain flour

1/2 cup (60 g/2 oz) self-raising flour

1 cup (90 g/3 oz) desiccated coconut

1/2 cup (115 g/3¾ oz) firmly packed soft brown sugar

100 g (3⅓ oz) butter

Filling

30 g (1 oz) butter

2 tablespoons golden syrup

400 g (12⅔ oz) can sweetened condensed milk

Topping

150 g (4¾ oz) dark chocolate

40 g (1⅓ oz) butter

1 Preheat the oven to moderate 180°C (350°F/Gas 4). Line the base and sides of a shallow 28 x 18 cm (11 x 7 inch) rectangular tin with aluminium foil.

2 Sift the flours together into a medium bowl. Add the coconut and stir. Make a well in the centre.

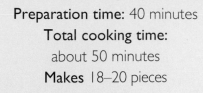

3 Combine the sugar and butter in a medium pan and stir over low heat until the butter has melted and the sugar has dissolved.

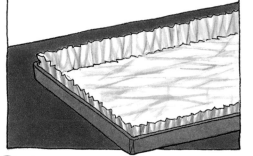

4 Pour the butter mixture into the dry ingredients and stir well to combine.

5 Press the mixture evenly onto the base of the prepared tin using the back of a spoon. Bake for 10 minutes then leave to cool.

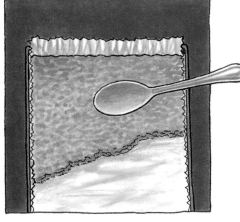

NOTE This slice can be stored in an airtight container for up to 4 days, if it lasts that long!

6 **To make Filling:** Combine the butter, syrup and condensed milk in a medium pan. Stir constantly over low heat using a wooden spoon until the butter has melted and the mixture is smooth. Continue stirring for about 10 minutes, until the mixture boils and lightly browns.

7 Pour this mixture over the pastry base and bake for 20 minutes. Remove from the oven and cool completely.

8 **To make Topping:** Place the chocolate and butter into a small heatproof bowl and stand it over a small pan of simmering water. Stir until the chocolate and butter have melted and the mixture is smooth.

9 Spread this mixture evenly over the caramel and allow to completely set. Using the foil, lift the slice from the tin and cut it into bars or squares to serve.

WAFFLES WITH CARAMEL SAUCE

Preparation time: 25 minutes
Total cooking time:
20 minutes
Makes 8 waffles

2 cups (250 g/8 oz) self-raising flour

1 teaspoon bicarbonate of soda

2 teaspoons sugar

2 eggs

90 g (3 oz) butter, melted

$1^3/_4$ cups (440 ml/14 fl oz) buttermilk

Caramel Sauce

100 g ($3^1/_3$ oz) butter

1 cup (185 g/6 oz) lightly packed soft brown sugar

$^1/_2$ cup (125 ml/4 fl oz) cream

1 Preheat a waffle iron. Sift the flour and soda into a large bowl, then add the sugar and stir to combine.

2 Whisk the eggs, butter and buttermilk together in a jug. Make a well in the centre of the dry ingredients, and pour in the egg mixture.

3 Whisk together gently until just smooth, cover with plastic wrap and set aside for 10 minutes.

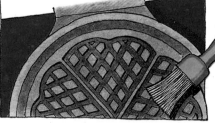

4 **To make Caramel Sauce:** Combine all the ingredients in a small pan. Stir over medium heat until the mixture is smooth; bring to the boil, reduce the heat slightly and simmer for 2 minutes. Set aside.

5 Brush the waffle iron with melted butter. Pour in $^1/_2$ cup (125 ml/4 fl oz) of batter, and quickly spread it out.

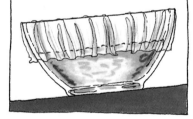

6 Close the lid and cook for about 2 minutes, or until crisp and golden. Repeat with the remaining mixture. Serve with vanilla ice cream and the Caramel Sauce.

CHOCOLATE TRUFFLES

1 Combine the butter and cream in a small pan. Stir over low heat until the butter has melted. Bring to the boil and remove from the heat immediately.

2 Place the chopped chocolate in a heatproof bowl and pour in the hot cream mixture. Cover the bowl for about 1 minute and then stir until the chocolate has melted and the mixture is completely smooth.

3 If you are adding any flavourings (see note), stir them in at this stage. Cool the mixture completely in the refrigerator.

5 Roll the balls in the grated chocolate. Place the truffles on a foil-lined tray and refrigerate until completely firm. These are delicious served with coffee. They will keep in an airtight container for at least 3 weeks.

4 When the mixture is firm enough to handle, roll heaped teaspoons into balls.

NOTE **To give your truffles a different flavour, add a couple of teaspoons of an 'essence' (these are very concentrated flavourings). Try vanilla, strawberry or orange essence. For a change, the truffles can be rolled in cocoa powder or drinking chocolate instead of the grated chocolate.**

Preparation time:
40 minutes + refrigeration
Total cooking time:
4 minutes
Makes about 24

★

50 g (1²/₃ oz) butter

¹/₃ cup (80 ml/2³/₄ fl oz) cream

250 g (8 oz) dark chocolate, chopped

100 g (3¹/₃ oz) dark, milk or white chocolate, grated

CHOC-MARSHMALLOW BITES

Preparation time:
20 minutes
Total cooking time:
3–4 minutes
Makes about 25 pieces

★

400 g (12²/₃ oz) dark chocolate, chopped

250 g (8 oz) mixed coloured marshmallows

1 cup (160 g/5¼ oz) unsalted roasted peanuts

100 g (3¹/₃ oz) glacé cherries, halved

½ cup (45 g/1½ oz) desiccated coconut, optional

1 Line the base and sides of an 18 x 28 cm (7 x 11 inch) rectangular tin with foil or baking paper.

2 Place the chocolate in a medium heatproof bowl. Stand the bowl over a small pan of simmering water and stir until the chocolate has completely melted and is smooth. Remove the pan from the heat but leave the bowl over the pan to keep the chocolate soft.

3 Roughly spread about one-quarter of the melted chocolate over the base of the prepared tin. Place the marshmallows, nuts and cherries randomly over the chocolate and press lightly to stick; sprinkle the coconut over if using.

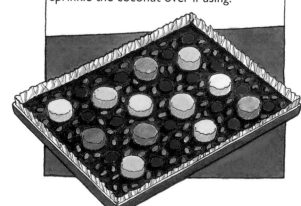

4 Pour the remaining chocolate evenly over the ingredients in the tin. Tap the tin on the bench to ensure the chocolate is evenly distributed between the gaps.

5 Refrigerate for 20 minutes, or until completely set. Carefully lift out of the tin. Remove the foil or paper and cut into pieces to serve. Refrigerate for up to 5 days.

ICED COFFEE

Preparation time:
15 minutes

Total cooking time: Nil

Serves 2

★

3–4 teaspoons instant coffee granules

1/3 cup (80 ml/2³/₄ fl oz) hot water

4 scoops vanilla ice cream

2¹/₂ cups (600 ml/20 fl oz) ice-cold milk

1¹/₄ cups (315 ml/10 fl oz) cream

drinking chocolate for dusting

1 Divide the coffee granules between 2 tall serving glasses. Adjust the amount of coffee used according to taste. If you like it stronger, add a little more.

2 Divide the water evenly, pouring it into each glass to dissolve the coffee.

3 Place 2 scoops of ice cream in each glass. Pour the cold milk over the ice cream.

4 Whip the cream until firm peaks form and carefully spoon or pipe on top. Dust with a little drinking chocolate and serve immediately.

NOTE **You may prefer to use freshly brewed or plunger coffee. Make a small, very strong pot. Refrigerate until really cold. Pour into the glasses and top with remaining ingredients. The coffee can also be made using all milk. Heat the milk in a pan until almost boiling, pour into the plunger with the ground coffee, then plunge. Pour into a jug and chill.**

HOT CHOCOLATE

Preparation time: 10 minutes
Total cooking time:
3–5 minutes
Serves 2

★

milk

drinking chocolate

marshmallows and grated
chocolate, optional

3 Carefully pour the hot milk into the mugs. Spoon 2–3 teaspoons of drinking chocolate into each mug. Adjust the quantity according to your taste. Mix well to dissolve the chocolate.

1 Fill 2 mugs with milk to determine the quantity needed.

2 Pour the milk into a medium pan and gently heat until almost boiling. Be careful not to let the milk boil over.

4 Place a couple of marshmallows on top, sprinkle with some grated chocolate and serve immediately.

NOTE You can use grated chocolate or cocoa powder as an alternative to drinking chocolate. Use about 2–3 tablespoons of grated chocolate per cup. If using cocoa, you may need to add a little sugar to sweeten.
This recipe can also be made in the microwave. Heat the milk in the mugs for about 45 seconds to 1 minute on High (100%). The time may vary slightly, according to your microwave wattage.

INDEX

This edition published in 2003 by Bay Books, an imprint of Murdoch Magazines Pty Limited, GPO Box 1203, Sydney NSW 2001.

This flip edition first published in 2002. Reprinted 2003.

ISBN 1 8977 30 49 7

A catalogue record of this book is available from the British Library.

Editorial Director: Susan Tomnay
Concept and Design: Marylouise Brammer
Managing Editor: Jane Price
Editors: Jane Bowring, Justine Upex
Illustrations: Mike Gorman
Food Editors: Roslyn Anderson, Kerrie Ray, Tracy Rutherford
Design Assistant: Jo Grey
Photographer: Luis Martin
Stylists: Rosemary Mellish
Food Preparation: Tracey Port, Dimitra Stais
Picture Librarian: Denise Martin
UK adaptation: Laura Jackson, Angela Newton

Chief Executive: Juliet Rogers
Publisher: Kay Scarlett

Printed by Imago Publishing in Thailand.

Murdoch Books UK Ltd
Ferry House, 51–57 Lacy Road
Putney, London SW15 1PR
United Kingdom
Tel: +44 (0)20 8355 1480
Fax: +44 (0)20 8355 1499
Murdoch Books UK Ltd is a subsidiary
of Murdoch Magazines Pty Ltd.

UK Distribution
Macmillan Distribution Ltd
Houndsmills, Brunell Road
Basingstoke, Hampshire, RG1 6XS
United Kingdom
Tel: +44 (0) 1256 302 707
Fax: +44 (0) 1256 351 437
http://www.macmillan-mdl.co.uk

Murdoch Books®
GPO Box 1203
Sydney NSW 2001
Australia
Tel: (612) 4352 7000
Fax: (612) 4352 7026
Murdoch Books® is a trademark
of Murdoch Magazines Pty Ltd.

INTERNATIONAL GLOSSARY

choc bits	chocolate drops/chips/morsels
rice bubbles	rice krispies
sultanas	seedless raisins/golden raisins
tomato paste	tomato purée, double concentrate